This Mac Is Mine

This Mac Is Mine

John Pivovarnick

 Addison-Wesley Publishing Company

Reading, Massachusetts • Menlo Park, California
New York • Don Mills, Ontario • Wokingham, England
Amsterdam • Bonn • Sydney • Singapore • Tokyo
Madrid • San Juan • Paris • Seoul • Milan
Mexico City • Taipei

Many of the designations used by manufacturers and sellers to distinguish their products are claimed as trademarks. Where those designations appear in this book and Addison-Wesley was aware of a trademark claim, the designations have been printed in initial capital letters.

The authors and publishers have taken care in preparation of this book and software package, but make no expressed or implied warranty of any kind and assume no responsibility for errors or omissions. No liability is assumed for incidental or consequential damages in connection with or arising out of the use of the information or programs contained herein.

Library of Congress Cataloging-in-Publication Data

Pivovarnick, John.
   This Mac is mine / John Pivovarnick.
     p. cm.
   ISBN 0-201-63206-3
   1. Macintosh (Computer)   I. Title.
  QA76.8.M3P58   1992
  004.165--dc20   92-10937
                                         CIP

Sponsoring Editor: Julie Stillman
Project Editor: Elizabeth Rogalin
Production Coordinator: Vicki Hochstedler
Technical Reviewers: Jane Tamlyn-Hayden and Langston Earley
Cover Design: Jean Seal
Cover Illustrations: Jeff Seaver
Set in 11-point Meridien by CIP

1 2 3 4 5 6 7 8 9-MW-9695949392
First printing, July 1992

For Langston

The Usual Suspects

In the tradition of most first books, it's time to round up the usual suspects and pass out thanks.

Thanks to my parents, for giving me my first computer, and my sister, Mary Ellen, for not creaming her little brother *every* chance she got. Thanks to my brother, Mike, who in 1985 said "Check this out. It's a Macintosh." *Now* look what you did.

Other folks who offered support and encouragement: The Darlings (Dawn, Brian, and those amazing McGurl boys), Teresa Fallon, and T. Greenfield especially. Also Claudia Earley-Stanford, Cathy Lyman, Sandy Lauro, and Juanita Epps.

Thanks also to all the software authors who graciously allowed me to cobble their work together to make something of my own. My work would mean nothing without theirs. Special thanks to Robert Johnston, who hustled his buns getting version 1.2 of WindowShade ready for release.

Thanks to Mark Carter (aka Pilobolus and Guide MC) for test driving some cranky chapters for me. I consider us friends, though we've never met outside of cyberspace.

Finally, thanks to Julie Stillman, Elizabeth Rogalin, and all the good folks at Addison-Wesley (this means you, Claire and Jane), for giving the new guy a chance.

I thank you one and all, but this one's for Langston Earley, my partner and the power behind the throne. Langston, who encouraged and helped, read crappy drafts of chapters, and listened to me alternately whine and snarl for three very long months.

I couldn't have done it without you, big guy.

Contents

Contents

Introduction

In which we discover the mysteries of Macintosh customization, and how
This Mac Is Mine *will help.*

Time was, if you wanted to imprint your personality on your computer, you bought a plant to set near it, or maybe pictures of your loved ones, or some toys. You know, like Whoopi Goldberg did in *Jumpin' Jack Flash.* I know one woman who painted her PC so it looked like the bus on "The Partridge Family." That's okay as far as it goes, but when you're done, it's still the same old computer behind all that froufrou.

For those poor souls stuck with DOS machines, that's about as good as it gets unless you start messing with GEOWorks Ensemble or Microsoft Windows. Even then your customizing options are limited.

But the Mac...now that's a different story. Macintosh computers are almost infinitely adaptable. Instead of just sprucing up the outside, you can get right down inside a Mac. Given the time and resources, you can customize just about everything. A little software here, a little shareware there, and every time you power up, your computer says, "This Mac is *mine."*

My own Mac's got a custom startup screen, custom icons, and souped up sounds. There's also a big ol' clock up on the menu bar, so I don't lose track of the time. That comes in handy when I'm using an online service and paying by the hour or the minute. All that plus other add-ins, *plus* the usual toy and picture accessories on the outside.

Given the Mac's adaptability, it's amazing how few people take up the gauntlet and make their Macs their own. If you're like most people, you probably haven't done much beyond changing the desktop pattern. Granted, unless you have a modem and want to spend a lot of time downloading the INITs, DAs, and control panels to customize your Mac, you'll probably just stick with changing the desktop pattern and (if you have a color monitor) the color options. If you're very new to the Macintosh, you may not even know how custom customized can be.

I'm here to tell you that you can make your Mac completely your own, a one-of-a-kind expression of your personality, and to give you the tools to get you started.

Overview

This Mac Is Mine is a customizing resource. The information in these pages and the software on the disk are the starting points for your own quest for the perfect desktop. Since customizing, by definition, is personal, I can't tell you what to do, just what you *can* do. These are options, not absolutes.

To make things a little easier, the book covers three areas:

Chapter Two talks about the customizing options you have right out of the box, using nothing more than your Mac's system software. Since System 7 hasn't (I suspect) captured everyone's attention yet, both Systems 6.0.7 and 7 are covered.

Chapters Three through Eleven deal specifically with installing, using, and playing around with the software included on the disk. Where you need something, like a graphic image or a sound file, to explore a particular program, there are some included as well. There are also hints, tips, and general advice about using the programs and advice about customizing your Mac in general. The great thing about advice is, you don't have to follow it if you don't want to.

Chapter Twelve contains additional resources, places you can go to get even more software, images, doodads, and whatnots, so you can create the ultimate custom desktop.

Basic Assumptions

As with any book that deals with computers, there are some basic assumptions at work here. While the text is geared toward beginning to intermediate Mac users, I assume that you have the Mac basics under your belt. You've read your manuals and know about pointing, clicking, dragging, and opening files, as well as closing, copying, and such.

If any of these terms are alien to you, *run*, do not walk, to the *Macintosh Reference* manual that came with your Mac and brush up.

While I'm in a disclaimer frame of mind, I should say (with apologies to Lily Tomlin), "I am not a hacker, but a real person like yourself." If you held a gun to my head, I could not write any of the software on the enclosed disk. I hold the folks who write good software in the highest regard.

Software falls into three general categories: commercial products, freeware, and shareware.

Commercial products are the packaged stuff you find in your local computer store. Buying it and opening the license-agreement envelope gives you the right to use it and make a copy for your archives. You rarely get to try it before you buy it, at least not in any serious way. Because you're paying for packaging, marketing, and glossy manuals, commercial software is expensive. If you don't like it, unless it came with a money-back guarantee, you're stuck

Freeware, like some of the software here, is just what it sounds like: free. You get it from electronic bulletin boards, some dealers, friends, wherever. It doesn't cost you anything except the blank disk and the time to find it or download it. If you don't like it, you haven't lost much.

Shareware, on the other hand, combines the best of both. It's software you have to pay a fee for, but it's usually very little (from $2 to $50), and a whole lot less than you'd pay for a commercial product. The best thing is, *you get to try it first*. You actually have full use of the program for a few weeks so you can decide whether or not it's what you want or need. If you like it and keep it, you're on your honor to send the author his or her requested fee. If you don't like it, you should erase it or pass it along to someone who might like it. Who says honor is dead?

For the shareware items included here, if you keep and use them, you are expected to pay the fees. Each shareware offering includes the information on how much and where to send the requested fee (either in a read-me file or as part of the program). Please do. It encourages shareware authors to upgrade their existing programs and to dream up some more.

Speaking as a nonhacker (as most of us are), we really need these folks who can write both serious applications and fun excess-ories (and the stuff in between) for the machines we've come to love. Don't discourage them.

Using the Disk

The first thing we have to do is kill all the lawyers...no, sorry! That's Shakespeare. The first thing *we* have to do is make a copy of the disk and put the original in a safe place. That's a good rule of thumb whenever you buy new software.

Copying the disk can save you a world of hurt later on if something untoward happens, like a child decides to slap a refrigerator magnet on your disk file or wants to play Mr. Wizard and see what happens to plastic in a microwave. Or the dog eats it. Stranger things have been known to happen. Play it safe. Copy your disk. If you don't know how to copy a disk, check the "Managing Disks and Drives" section of the *Macintosh Reference* manual that came with your Mac. I'll wait.

Once your original is tucked away in a safe place, turn on your Mac (if you haven't already). When the desktop appears, insert the locked duplicate disk in your drive and double-click on its icon.

Decompressing the Disk

The *This Mac Is Mine* disk contains over 1.2 megabytes of assorted applications, graphics, read-me files, and other stuff. Through the magic of technology, it's all crammed onto an 800K disk.

The programs were compressed using Bill Goodman's excellent **Compact Pro 1.32,** a shareware compression utility that mashes files down to about half their original size. It's a self-extracting archive, which means you don't have to own Compact Pro to get at its contents. (For more information on acquiring shareware, check out Chapter 12 and the Reference List at the end of this book.)

To decompress the archive, just double-click on its icon. You'll be presented with the dialog shown in Figure 1-1. It allows you to select where everthing will land after decompression. When it finishes, there will be a new folder on your hard drive called Mac/Mine Apps. Select your hard drive, since the contents won't fit on a high density disk. Click on **Extract**, and Compact Pro does its thing. It will take a few minutes; there's a lot of stuff for it to go through.

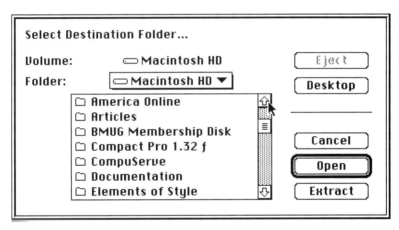

Figure 1-1. Compact Pro Screen

Everything in the Mac/Mine folder is organized by program. Each program has its own folder which contains documentation and accessory files (like sounds and images) that are appropriate to the program. There's an additional file of images called Picture Files, that will come in handy later—no peeking.

Compatibility Notes

You know the old saying, You can't please everybody. Well, it's true. You can't. I know, I've tried.

There is something for every Mac owner on the *This Mac Is Mine* disk, but everything isn't for everyone. Some programs will run on any Mac (GIFConverter, Sound Mover, StartupSndInit, SndControl, WindowShade, Desktop Notes). Another, Colorize, requires a color Mac. Still others are meant for use with System 7 only (NoBalloonMenu), or System 6.0.7 and earlier (Layout). See the compatibility chart at the back of the book for more complete information.

I know there's an unwritten Mac-law that says manuals are for weenies, but do yourself a favor and at least skim through the chapters relating to these programs before you try them on your system.

Bugs, Disclaimers, and Such

I've used everything on this disk. So have others with varying degrees of Mac savvy. To the best of our knowledge, everything works by itself and with some or all of the others, but there's no way to predict every combination of hardware and software out there.

INIT conflicts happen. Odd bugs crop up on different machines in different configurations. Sometimes you just have a bad day.

Beyond making the statement, "If it bombed out on me, I didn't include it here," I make no claims about the performance of the software on the enclosed disk. Use it at your own risk.

If you encounter a conflict, check the INIT Management 101 section in Chapter 12. It contains hints and strategies for getting around INIT conflicts.

If you discover a bug, report it to the program's author. Many of the program documentation and read-me files contain information on how to contact the authors.

Hey, contact them even if you don't find a bug. Good news and compliments are always welcome, as are shareware fees.

Mac Basics

In which young Pip discovers that Nancy Reagan isn't really the mother of us all, and the one-armed man shows him how to customize his Mac interface with only his system software, two rubber bands, and a paper clip.

Welcome to Macintosh!

Even if you bought your Macintosh computer five years ago, you probably remember the thrill you got when you first put it together and fired it up. There's nothing like the feeling of a new computer coming to life.

Unfortunately, you also may have been disappointed after you poked around in the system software. On the face of it, the system software doesn't appear to be that interesting. After all, it's just a bunch of utilities for copying, moving, and trashing files. Sure, there are some fun features, like the Calculator and the Puzzle, but how often are you going to use them?

You may have been daunted by the shorthand you have to learn to talk about the system: INITs, CDEVS, RDEVS, and DAs. Instead of learning a little about what these nicknames stand for and what they do, most people prefer to get into applications right away and actually "do something" with their new computer. That's unfair to the Mac's system software.

No other operating system I'm aware of lets you add, delete, or customize features with as little fuss as the Macintosh does. Nor does any system have the number of tools that the Mac has, to let you add and further customize features the way you can with a Mac.

Even working on a new Macintosh, with only the System disks and your native wit, you still have a variety of customizing options to play with. Most of these are available when you select the **Control Panel** (or **Control Panels** in System 7) option under the menu.

To keep everything simple, we'll only look at the most recent versions of the Mac's system software, System 6.0.7 and System 7. To cover *all* the system variations would take too long. If you want to customize a Mac running System 6.0.5 or earlier, check the manual that came with your System disks. A lot of what follows may apply, but a lot may not.

If you aren't sure what version of the Mac's system software you're running, you can check it under the menu in the Finder (or MultiFinder). When you click on the menu if the first entry is "About this Macintosh," you're running System 7. If it reads "About the Finder," you're running System 6 or earlier. To find out the exact version number, select **About the Finder**. The dialog box will tell you, in no uncertain terms, which version of the Mac's system software you have running.

A Word about Color

In this book, you'll find references to all sorts of colors: highlight colors, desktop pattern colors, window colors, and more. If you own a Mac with a built-in black-and-white monitor, a lot of this won't apply. You might want to skip ahead to Chapter Three.

If, when you use your system software or a program from the disk, a color option doesn't appear or behaves differently from what's described here, don't panic. That means your system isn't able to make use of a color function or uses it another way.

If you have a grayscale or paper-white monitor, please translate "color" to "shades of gray," or whatever is appropriate for your display. For simplicity, I'll use the term "color" for all cases.

Customizing System 6.0.7

Under the menu (Figure 2-1), selecting the **Control Panel** option brings up the Control Panel window (Figure 2-2). There you can select any of the system features that are available for customization. Using the scrollbar to the left of the window, you can scroll through the various controls. These include the **General**, **Color**, **Keyboard**, **Mouse**, and **Sound** Control Panels. Clicking on an icon brings up that control panel.

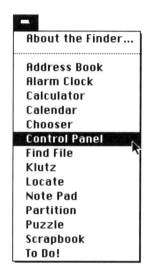

Figure 2-1. Apple Menu

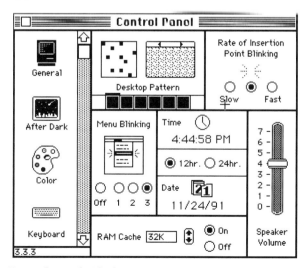

Figure 2-2. Control Panel Window

The Keyboard and Mouse controls should be set to accommodate your level of typing and clicking expertise. Set them however you prefer.

When you first open the Control Panel, you're automatically at the General controls.

General Controls

The Date, Time, and Blink (both Insertion Point and Menu) settings are a matter of personal preference. Likewise, you prefer either the 12-hour or the 24-hour time display. As far as either of the blink rates is concerned, work with each of the settings until you find the one that's right for you.

The RAM (random access memory) cache setting determines how much memory the system sets aside for storing temporary data. Because your Mac doesn't have to access a disk constantly to read information already stored in the cache, it works faster. If you have tons of memory (4 megs or more), you can set up a generous cache without problems. If you have a limited amount of RAM, try various settings until you find one that helps more than it hinders you. Out of memory messages, which vary from system to system, let you know if you've been too generous with the RAM cache.

Speaker volume is as much a matter of courtesy as personal preference. I share office space (with a PC consultant, but I don't hold it against him). The Mac's beep, at full volume can drive someone working in the same room to distraction. Add some other sounds (as we will with **SndControl**) and it can get annoying—trust me on this. We'll deal with sound in more detail later. For now, set your volume at a level that's comfortable for you and those around you.

The most fun you can have with the General controls is changing the desktop pattern.

Desktop Patterns

If you click on the left and right arrow keys over the miniature desktop sample (Figure 2-3), you can flip through the patterns that come preloaded in the system. To try them on your desktop, click on the miniature desktop. The new pattern replaces the old one.

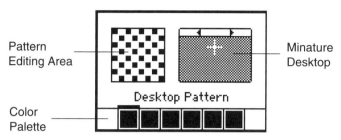

Figure 2-3. Desktop Pattern Area

If you don't like any of the sample patterns, you can change them to something you do like. It's easy to overwrite the samples. Just click on one of the eight colors at the bottom of the pattern area to select it. A thick black box surrounds the active color.

Move the crosshair cursor over the pattern editing area and click away. The editing area is essentially an eight-by-eight, magnified view of the pattern you're creating. When you click on one of the squares, it turns the selected color. Click on the square again, and it reverts to the previous color.

As you make changes in the pattern, you'll see them appear in the miniature desktop, giving you an on-the-fly look as the pattern develops.

Think of the editing area as a single floor tile. The full desktop is the floor you want to cover. As you get better at seeing how the tiles fit into the overall desktop pattern, you'll be able to design tiles that interconnect, and you'll be able to create desktop patterns more intricate than the individual tiles, like the bubble pattern shown in Figure 2-4.

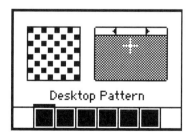 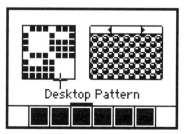

Figure 2-4 Sample Desktop Patterns

11

Changing Palettes

If you don't like the color palette assigned to a sample pattern, you can create your own custom palette. Just double-click on the color you want to change. That calls up the color picker, shown in Figure 2-5. Its real name is the Color-wheel dialog box. It lets you pick the eight colors, one at a time, for your custom palette.

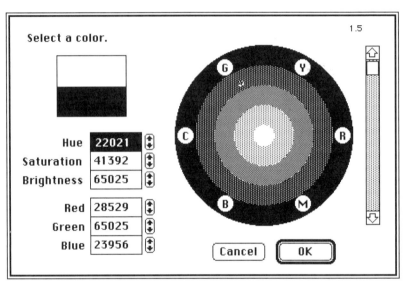

Figure 2-5. The Color-Wheel Dialog Box

When you first call up the color wheel, the active color fills the square in the upper left corner of the dialog box. A small black circle shows where the current color is on the color wheel. You change the color by moving the cursor onto the color wheel (the cursor changes to a circle) and clicking on the desired color. The new color shows in the top half of the Select a color square so you can compare it to the old one.

Once you select a color, you can modify it further with the brightness control scroll bar beside the color wheel. The top of the bar is the brightest; the bottom is darkest and turns everything black. You can tweak the color even more by changing the values in the Hue/Saturation/Brightness and Red/Green/Blue boxes, below the Select a color square.

When you're satisfied with the new color, click on the **OK** button. The new color replaces the old one in the palette. Repeat the process for each color you want to change.

Changing the palette changes the minature desktop pattern. After changing colors, you don't have to go in and edit the pattern. The new color replaces all occurrences of the old color in the miniature desktop pattern.

After you've created your desktop pattern masterpiece, click on the miniature desktop to replace the current pattern with your new one.

A word of warning: Once you've customized the desktop pattern, you can't try any other pattern on the desktop unless you first save your custom pattern by double-clicking on the minature desktop. Then you can edit new patterns, but if you don't double-click on the miniature desktop to save it, you will erase your custom pattern from memory and have to start over.

Highlights

Once you've set the desktop pattern, you can use the Color Control Panel to select a coordinated highlight color. Using the icon scrollbar, scroll until you see the Color icon. Click on it to open the Color Control Panel shown in Figure 2-6.

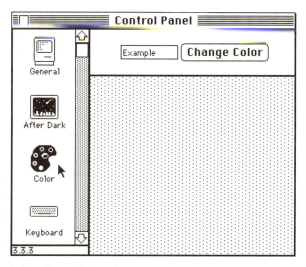

Figure 2-6. Color Control Panel

The only option you have here is changing the highlight color. That's how the Mac shows which icon is selected on the desktop or in a window. Other applications, like word processors, use the highlight color to show selected text in a document.

The Example box displays the current highlight color. To change it, click on the **Change Color** button beside it. This calls up the same color-wheel dialog we used to change the palette for our desktop pattern in Figure 2-5. The only difference is, instead of Select a color, it now says Select a highlight color. Pick your new highlight color. Adjust it as you wish with the brightness slider and the controls below the color square. When you're done, click on the **OK** button or press Return.

Sound Advice

We've dealt with the Mac's visual elements (patterns and color). Now let's play with the aural part of the Mac interface. You open the Sound Control Panel like any other, by clicking on its icon in the scroll window. That calls up the control panel shown in Figure 2-7. Here you have the option of adjusting the volume of the Mac's speaker with the Speaker Volume control. You can also choose an alert sound. The basic system choices include: Simple Beep, Clink-Klank, Boing, and Monkey. Clicking on the name plays the sound, and the names conveniently evoke the sounds.

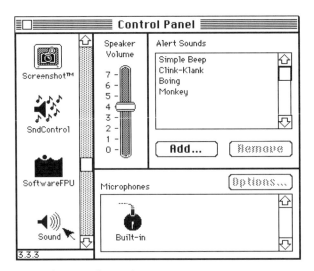

Figure 2-7. Sound Control Panel

After listening to them, click on the one you want for your alert sound. Your Mac uses the alert sound to tell you it doesn't like something you do (such as press an inappropriate key combination), or needs information (insert another disk), or wants to second-guess you (Are you sure you want to do that?).

If you're new to the Macintosh, you're going to hear that sound *a lot,* until you get the hang of working with it. Be sure to pick a sound you like, at least one that won't annoy you.

If your Mac has sound input capability (a fancy way of saying it comes with a microphone), then you have the option of adding your own system sounds.

For those who don't have a microphone, you might want to skip ahead to Chapter Four. **Sound Mover,** on the enclosed disk, comes with an assortment of sounds you can add without a microphone.

Grow Your Own Sounds

To use your Mac's microphone to add a sound to the Alert Sounds list, click on the **Add** button below the sound window. This opens a window that looks amazingly like the controls on a tape recorder (Figure 2-8). Not only does it look like a tape recorder, it works like one too.

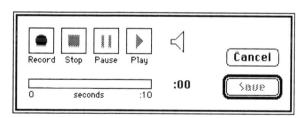

Figure 2-8. Record Dialog

When you're ready to record a sound (make sure your microphone is plugged into the audio-in jack), click on the **Record** button. The microphone will pick up any kind of sound you can produce. When you're done, click on the **Stop** button. It's that simple.

If you want to have several sounds play in sequence in the same alert, you can. Click on **Record**, and sample the first sound, then click on **Pause.** Prepare the second sound and, when you're ready to continue, click on **Pause** again. Recording resumes. You can repeat the process until you've used the ten seconds allotted for alert sounds.

To listen to your new sound, click on the **Play** button. The sound plays through your Mac's speaker.

If you're not happy with the sound, you can repeat the recording process, which tapes over the old sound. If you like the new sound, click on the **Save** button.

When you click on the **Save** button, the Save Sound dialog appears (see Figure 2-9). Type in an appropriate name (something to help you remember what the sound is) and click on **OK**. Your sound is saved and now appears in the Alert Sounds window. It can be selected, deselected, or removed like any other sound (except the Simple Beep, which cannot be removed).

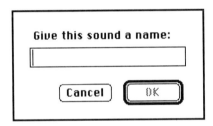

Figure 2-9. Save Sound Dialog

You can use sounds from other audio sources as well.

The box that contains your microphone also has an odd-looking widget with a microphone jack (plug) on one end and a box with two RCA-type receptacles on the other. This is the phono-plug adapter, which allows you to feed stereo audio-out signals from your stereo tuner, cassette deck, CD player, VCR, or whatever, into your Mac (in mono only) (see Figure 2-10).

Just take your left and right audio-out leads from your audio source and plug them into the two RCA receptacles at the large end of the phono-plug adapter. It doesn't matter which plug goes where because the adapter blends the channels (left and right) into one. Then, remove the regular microphone jack from the back of your Mac and plug in the jack end of the adapter. You're ready to go.

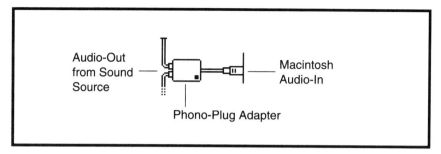

Figure 2-10. Phono-Plug Adapter

It takes coordination and some practice to get the timing right in starting your sound source and then clicking on the **Record** button, but it's worth the effort. You can add some really wild sounds to your Mac. Anything from bits of a favorite song to sound effects to scraps of dialog from your favorite movie (like HAL saying, "Dave, we have a problem," in *2001: A Space Odyssey*). As long as you have the patience and the disk space (sounds take up a lot of room), the sky's the limit.

Wrapping Up System 6.0.7

So, there are the customizing features of System 6.0.7. Some for touch, some for sight, some for sound. They give you the flexibility to make your Mac your own, but not so much that your Mac is completely unique. That's where the *This Mac Is Mine* disk comes in.

If you have no interest in checking out the new and improved customizing features of System 7, skip ahead to the next chapter. Be sure you read and follow the installation instructions carefully. Also read the operating instructions for each program *before* you try them. Nothing included here will physically injure your Mac, but improper use can cause some nasty crashes that I'm sure you'd rather avoid.

By the Way...

If you're sitting on the fence about upgrading to System 7 (you don't want to shell out money for additional memory and software upgrades, don't want to give up your incompatible software, whatever) you can run System 7 along with an earlier version with little or no hassle.

You can install System 7 on a separate partition of your hard drive and then switch between system versions using the Set Startup function under the Special menu in the Finder or MultiFinder. The caveat here is that it must be a *real* partition formatted into your hard drive with a utility like La Cie's **Silverlining**. A pseudo-partition, like the big, invisible folder created when you use the Partition desk accessory included with Central Point's **MacTools Deluxe**, won't work.

If you'd rather not deal with changing the Startup option and restarting your Mac often, there are programs to make switching between system versions less of a chore. One is the **SwitchBoot INIT**, which lets you indicate which volume and partition you want to boot from as you're starting up. Another is **System Picker**, which lets you do much the same thing.

If that's entirely too much to deal with (backing up your hard drive, partitioning, restoring everything to one partition, and installing System 7 in the other partition) you can run both without partitioning. It's still work, but it's not a lot of work. Here's how:

- First, make a backup of your hard drive. You should always have a current backup before you start messing with your System Folder.

- Next, rename your current System Folder. The new name should remind you immediately of what's in there. I call mine Old System (*duh*). To change the name, just click on your System Folder and type the new name.

- Now create a new folder (using the New Folder option under the File menu). Name it Finder Hider or something similar. You're going to hide the Finder in it.

- Once that's done, double-click on the old System Folder (whatever you've named it) and locate the Finder icon. Click and drag the Finder icon out of the old System folder and into the new Finder Hider folder. Your old system is deactivated.

- Select **Restart** from the Special menu. When the System bell sounds, insert the Install 1 disk from set of ten (!) 800K disks that make up System 7. Your Mac will boot from the floppy, and then you can simply follow the installation instructions from there on out. When you finish, restart your Mac (using Restart, from the Special menu) and you'll start up in System 7.

- Later, when you want to switch between systems, return the Finder icon to the currently deactivated System Folder. Next remove the Finder icon from the currently active System Folder (as you did above), and restart your Mac. Make sure that the system acknowledges the change of Finders by placing the small Mac icon on the newly activated System Folder, called Blessing the System Folder. If it doesn't, reopen the folder and click/drag the Finder icon a little bit. Leave it selected when you close the window.

- Remember: You can't have *both* versions of your system active at the same time. That's a bad thing. Your Mac won't explode, but it won't be very happy with you; it will bomb, freeze, or otherwise announce its displeasure.

That's a freebie, no additional software required, just a little electronic elbow grease.

Customizing System 7

Under System 7, there are several ways to get at the Mac's customizing features. By pulling down the ⌘ menu (Figure 2-11), you can select the **Control Panels** option to open the Control Panels window (Figure 2-12). You can also double-click on the Control Panels folder, if you are already in the System Folder. Or you can make an alias of the Control Panels folder and leave it on the desktop at all times. (See your System 7 manual for more information on aliasing.) The catch word for System 7 is convenience.

However you get to it, you begin in the Control Panels window. There you can select the feature you want to customize just by double-clicking on its icon. The window contains icons for the **General Controls**, **Color**, **Keyboard**, **Labels**, **Mouse**, **Memory**, **Sound**, **and Views** Control Panels.

Figure 2-11. Apple Menu

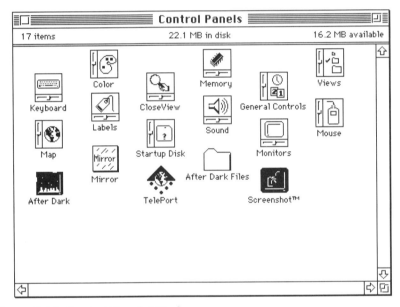

Figure 2-12. Control Panels Window

The Keyboard and Mouse controls should be set to accommodate to your level of typing and clicking expertise. Set them however you prefer.

The Memory Control Panel sets the RAM (random access
memory) Disk cache. It lets you specify how much memory the
system sets aside for storing temporary data. Because your Mac
doesn't have to access a disk constantly to read information stored

in the cache, it works faster. If you have tons of memory (4 megs or more), you can set up a generous cache without problems. If you have a limited amount of RAM, try various settings until you find one that helps more than it hinders you. The out of memory messages let you know if you've been too generous with the RAM cache.

You also use the Memory Control Panel to toggle 32-bit Addressing and Virtual Memory on and off. They are specific to certain Macintosh models. If your Mac can't use them, they won't even appear in the control panel. Consult your System 7 manual if you feel the need to adjust these advanced memory features.

Let's start with General Controls by double-clicking on its icon in the Control Panels window.

General Controls

The Date, Time, and Blink (both Insertion Point and Menu) settings are a matter of personal preference. Likewise, you either prefer the 12-hour or the 24-hour time display. As far as either of the blink rates is concerned, work with each of the settings until you find the one that's right for you.

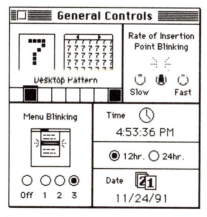

Figure 2-13. General Controls Panel

The most fun you can have with the General Controls is changing the desktop pattern. If you click on the left and right arrow keys over the miniature desktop sample (Figure 2-14), you can flip through the patterns that come preloaded in the system. To try them on your desktop, click on the miniature desktop. The new pattern replaces the old one.

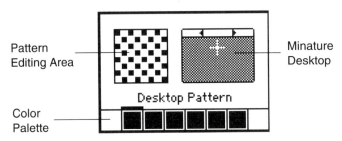

Figure 2-14. Desktop Pattern Area

If you don't like any of the sample patterns, you can change them to something you do like. It's easy to overwrite the samples. Just click on one of the eight colors at the bottom of the pattern area to select it. A thick black box surrounds the active color.

Move the crosshair cursor over the pattern editing area and click away. It's essentially an eight-by-eight, magnified view of the pattern you're creating. When you click on one of the squares, it turns the selected color. Click on it again, and it reverts to the previous color.

As you make changes in the pattern, you'll see them appear in the miniature desktop, giving you an on-the-fly look as the pattern develops.

Think of the editing area as a single floor tile. The full desktop is the floor you want to cover. As you get better at seeing how the single tile fits into the overall desktop pattern, you'll be able to design tiles that interconnect, and you'll be able to create desktop patterns more intricate than the individual tiles, like the bubble pattern shown in Figure 2-15.

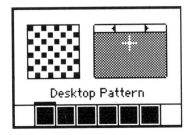 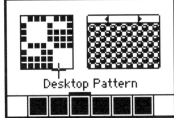

Figure 2-15. Sample Desktop Patterns

Changing Palettes

If you don't like the color palette for a sample pattern, you can create your own custom palette. Just double-click on the color you want to change. That calls up the color picker, as shown in Figure 2-16. Its real name is the Color-wheel dialog box. It lets you pick the eight colors, one at a time, for your custom palette.

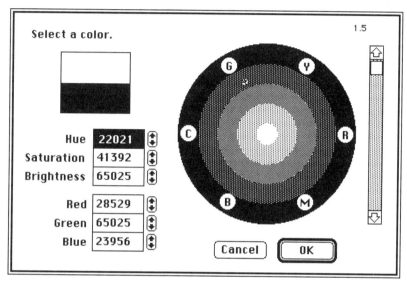

Figure 2-16. The Color-Wheel Dialog Box

When you first call up the color wheel, the active color fills the square in the upper left corner of the dialog. A small black circle shows where the current color is on the color wheel. You change the color by moving the cursor onto the color wheel (the cursor changes to a circle) and clicking on the desired color. The new color shows in the top half of the Select a color square so you can compare it to the old one.

Once you select a color, you can modify it further with the brightness control slider beside the color wheel. The top of the slide is brightest; the bottom is darkest and turns everything black. You can tweak the color even more by changing the values in the Hue/Saturation/Brightness and Red/Green/Blue boxes, below the Select a color square.

When you're satisfied with the new color, click on the **OK** button. The new color replaces the old one in the palette. Repeat the process for each color you want to change.

Changing the color palette changes the miniature desktop pattern. After changing colors, you don't have to edit the new colors into the pattern. The new color replaces all occurrences of the old color in the miniature desktop pattern.

After you've created your desktop pattern masterpiece, click on the miniature desktop to replace the current pattern with your new one.

A word of warning: Once you've customized the desktop pattern, you can't try another pattern on the desktop unless you first save your custom pattern by double-clicking on the miniature desktop. Then you can edit new patterns or flip through the sample patterns, but if you don't double-click on the miniature desktop and save it, you will erase your custom pattern from memory and have to start over.

Color Commentary

Once you've set the desktop pattern, you can use the Color Control Panel to select a coordinated highlight color. If the General Controls Panel is still open, click the close box in the upper left corner of the panel. You'll return to the Control Panels window.

Locate the Color icon and double-click on it to open the Color Control Panel (Figure 2-17). You have two options here: changing the Highlight and Window colors.

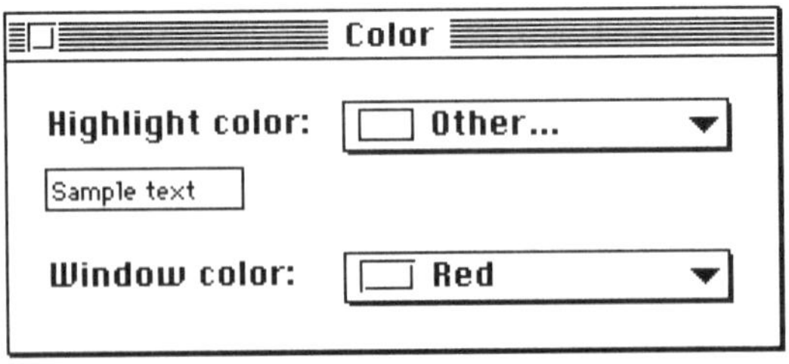

Figure 2-17. The Color Control Panel

The Mac uses the highlight color to show which icon is selected on the desktop or in a window. Other applications, like word processors, use the highlight color to show selected text in a document. The Sample text box displays the current highlight color.

Changing colors is easier under System 7; you don't have to deal with the color wheel for standard colors. If you click on the **Other** box to the right of Highlight color (see Figure 2-17), you're presented with a pop-up menu, which gives you an assortment of colors (see Figure 2-18). The last option, the Other... option, calls up the color-wheel dialog (Figure 2-16).

Figure 2-18. Highlight Color Menu

Figure 2-19. Window Color Menu

Likewise, when you click on the menu box next to **Window color**, you are presented with a pop-up menu of standard colors. You aren't given the option of selecting a nonstandard color. There is no Other... option for a custom window color—but hey! we never even had the option of color windows before.

Selecting a color from the Window color menu tints the menu bar, scroll arrows, and scroll bar in all of your windows. Check them out!

Sound Advice

We've dealt with the Mac's visual elements (patterns and color). Now let's play with the aural part of the Mac interface. You open the Sound Control Panel like any other. Double-click on its icon in the Control Panels window. That calls up the Sound Control Panel shown in Figure 2-20. You have the option of adjusting the volume of your Mac's speaker with the Speaker Volume control.

Speaker volume is as much a matter of courtesy as personal preference. I share office space (with a PC consultant, but I don't hold it against him). The Mac's beep at full volume can drive someone working in the same room to distraction. Add some other sounds (as we will with **SndControl**) and it can get annoying—trust me on this. We'll deal with sound in more detail later on. For now, set your volume at a level that's comfortable for you and those around you.

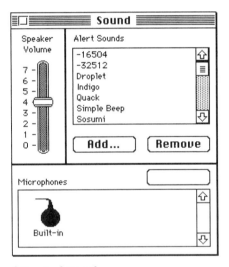

Figure 2-20. Sound Control Panel

You also have a choice of alert sounds: Droplet, Indigo, Quack, Simple Beep, Sosumi, or Wild Eep. Some of the sounds are obvious from their names. You can click on each sound name and hear it. Click on the one you want for your alert sound. Your Mac uses the alert sound to tell you it doesn't like something you do (such as press an inappropriate key combination), or needs information (insert another disk), or wants to second-guess you (Are you sure you want to do that?).

If you're new to the Macintosh, you're going to hear that sound *a lot,* until you get the hang of working with it. Be sure to pick a sound you like, at least one that won't annoy you.

If your Mac has sound input capability (a fancy way of saying a built-in microphone), then you have the option of adding your own system sounds. That's where the fun starts.

For those who don't have a microphone, you might want to skip ahead to Chapter Four. **Sound Mover**, on the enclosed disk, comes with an assortment of sounds you can add without a microphone.

Grow Your Own Sounds

To use your Mac's microphone to add a sound to the Alert Sounds list, click on the **Add** button below the sound window. This opens a window that looks amazingly like the controls on a tape recorder (Figure 2-21). Not only does it look like a tape recorder, it works like one too.

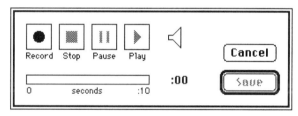

Figure 2-21. Record Dialog

When you're ready to record a sound (make sure the microphone is plugged into the audio-in jack), click on the **Record** button. The microphone will pick up any kind of sound you can produce. When you're done, click on the **Stop** button. It's that simple.

If you want to have more than one sound in the same alert, you can. Click on **Record**, and produce the first sound, then click on **Pause.** Prepare the second sound and, when you're ready to continue, click on **Pause** again. Recording resumes. You can repeat the process until you've used the ten seconds allotted for alert sounds.

To listen to your new sound, click on the **Play** button. The sound plays through your Mac's speaker.

If you're not happy with the sound, you can repeat the recording process, which tapes over the old sounds. If you like the new sound, click on the **Save** button.

When you click on the **Save** button, the Save Sound dialog appears (see Figure 2-22). Type in an appropriate name (something to help you remember what the sound is) and click on **OK**. Your sound is saved and appears in the Alert Sounds window. It can be selected, deselected, or removed like any other sound (except the Simple Beep, which cannot be removed).

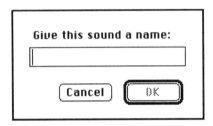

Figure 2-22. Save Sound Dialog

You can use sounds from other audio sources, as well.

The box that contains your microphone also has an odd looking widget with a microphone jack (plug) on one end and a box with two RCA-type receptacles on the other. This is called the phono-plug adapter, which allows you to feed stereo audio-out signals from your stereo tuner, cassette deck, CD player, or VCR, into your Mac (in mono only) (see Figure 2-23).

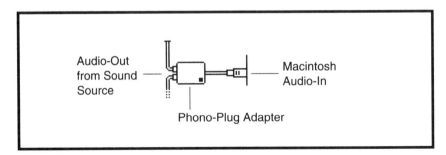

Figure 2-23. Phono-Plug Adapter

Just take your left and right audio-out leads from your audio source and plug them into the two RCA receptacles at the large end of the phono-plug adapter. It doesn't matter which plug goes where because the adapter blends the channels (left and right) into one. Then, remove the regular microphone jack from the back of your Mac and plug in the jack end of the adapter. You're ready to go.

It takes practice and some coordination to get the timing right in starting your sound source and then clicking on the **Record** button, but it's worth the effort. You can add some really wild sounds to your Mac. Anything from bits of a favorite song to sound effects to scraps of dialog from your favorite movie (like HAL saying, "Dave, we have a problem," in *2001: A Space Odyssey*). As long as you have the patience and the disk space (sounds take up a lot of room), the sky's the limit.

Neatly Labeled

There are a few brand-spanking-new customizing features available only with System 7 and a few improvements on old features. They'll be a real help in organizing your desktop, saving you both time and energy.

In the organizing department, there's the Labels menu. It's an improvement on the Color menu under System 6.0.7 and earlier versions.

Once, when you assigned a color to a desktop icon or folder, you had to rely on your memory to keep track of what the colors meant—something my own patchy memory could never do. With System 7, you can associate a word label with the color. The words let you make the label something meaningful, and they show up in the Label column when you list files by name (in the Views menu). No more wracking your brain for mnemonic devices to remind you of a color's significance.

The labels provided are generic, but useful even so. However, everything in the Labels menu (see Figure 2-24) can be tailored to suit your needs. You edit them through the Labels Control Panel (see Figure 2-25). Double-click on the Labels icon in the Control Panels window.

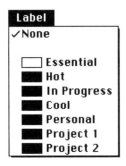

Figure 2-24. Label Menu
before Editing

Figure 2-25. Labels Control Panel
before Editing

Don't like an assigned color? Double-clicking on its box calls up the color wheel dialog (shown back in Figure 2-16). Select, adjust, and tweak a new color as you did when adjusting the highlight color or the desktop pattern palette. When you've chosen one, click on the **OK** button, and the new color replaces the old.

Don't like an assigned label? Double-click on the word and type a new one right over it. Change one or all of them. When you're done, close the control panel. Your changes take effect immediately (see Figure 2-26).

Figure 2-26. Labels Control Panel and Menu after Editing

To use the labels you've created, click on a file or folder to select it. While it's highlighted, pull down the Label menu and select the appropriate label. The selected file or folder's icon changes to the label color, and under the Label column (when you list files by name) your label-word appears, giving you two visual clues to the file's contents and importance (see Figure 2-27).

	Name	Size	Kind	Label	La
	Part One	59K	Symantec GreatWor...	Cool	
	Part One v2	30K	Symantec GreatWor...	Cool	
	Part One v3	41K	Symantec GreatWor...	Hot	
	Part Three	6K	Symantec GreatWor...	In Progress	
	PD Letter	5K	Symantec GreatWor...	–	
	Query Letter	10K	Symantec GreatWor...	–	
	Release form	4K	Symantec GreatWor...	–	
	Screen Shots	–	folder	In Progress	

This Mac/Mine MS — 17 items — 511K in disk — 894K available

Figure 2-27. Window with Labels

A View to a Folder

Labels make life easy when you're viewing files and folders by name. The Views Control Panel, shown in Figure 2-28, eases your eyes when you view by icon. Views lets you determine how your icons are arranged on the desktop. You can also specify icon size, as well as the size and font of the text beneath icons. Open the control panel by double-clicking on the Views icon.

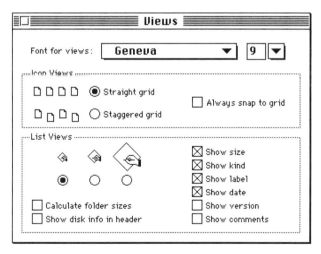

Figure 2-28. Views Control Panel

The Font for views box calls up a pop-up menu. Clicking on it lets you choose the font for all file and folder names. It can be any one of your installed fonts. Next to that, another pop-up menu lets you specify the display font's size.

If you ever had trouble reading filenames under older System versions, you'll love this feature.

The point sizes that appear in outline (for example, 14) look crispest on the screen with few or no jagged edges, but you can specify any available size. Experiment with combinations of fonts and sizes until you find the one that's best for you. Your tired eyes will thank you.

Icon Views lets you choose how files are arranged on the desktop—either in a straight line or staggered. If you use a large font or long filenames, staggering the layout eliminates most of the filename overlap. You can also select **Always snap to grid**, which moves a file to the closest grid space when you drag a file. You may find it annoying, you may not. Try it both ways for a while and choose the one you prefer.

Under List Views you have three choices of icon size and eight choices for the information you want displayed in list views. Depending on how you work and what information you need, try various combinations to see what fits your work style. Some options (like Calculate folder sizes) will slow your system down noticeably. Choose your views with care.

When you're done selecting your Views options, click on the close box. All the options you selected take effect immediately except Icon Views. To lay your folders out in the new grid pattern, select **Cleanup Window** from the **Special** menu. Then sit back and watch as your folders zip around the window into their new configuration. An example of a file window before and after cleanup is shown in Figures 2-29 and 2-30.

Holding down the Option key when you select the **Special** menu changes the Cleanup Window option to Cleanup by Name. Not only do your folders and files snap to their new grid pattern, they also land in alphabetical order. You can also use the View menu as a sorting and cleanup tool.

First select **View by Name**, which collapses your icon view to teeny-tiny icons followed by the filenames. Next select **View by Label**, **Date**, or **Version**. This sorts the filenames by your assigned label, the date you modified the files, or the program's version number.

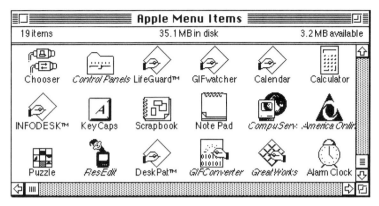

Figure 2-29. File Window before Cleanup

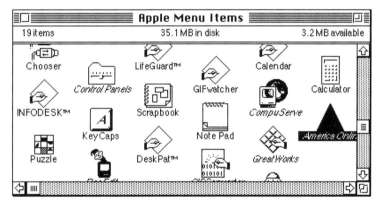

Figure 2-30. File Window after Cleanup

Now reselect **View by Icon** under the View menu. The file display returns to the large icon view as it was before, *but*, if you hold down the Option key while selecting the Special menu now, **Cleanup Window** becomes **Cleanup by Label**, **Date**, or **Version** (depending on which one you left active before returning to the icon view).

Other System 7 time-saving customizing features you might want to explore are use of aliases, which are file and application clones that you can leave on the desktop at all times or drop into the menu; adding desk accessories and application aliases to the menu without the Font/DA Mover; and the new networking options (if you're on a network). Check your System 7 manual for further information.

Miscellany

Two last things are worth mentioning about System 7. You can replace the icon of almost any document, folder, application, or disk with one of your own choosing, and you can put your own picture in the Puzzle desk accessory. Both are as easy as copy and paste.

To change the icon of a document or folder, first decide on the new icon. It can be anything that can be copied to the clipboard. Draw a new one in MacPaint, MacDraw, or any graphics program. You can also use a scanned photo, clip art from an art disk, or lift an icon from another program (like HyperCard's Art Bits stack).

Wherever you find it, copy your art to the clipboard by selecting it in the way that's appropriate for the program you're using. Then select **Copy** from the Edit menu. Return to the Finder (if you're still in a program) and click on the icon you want to change. Use the **Get Info** command under the File menu. Click on the icon in the Info Box (a box appears around it) and select **Paste** from the Edit menu. The new icon replaces the old. Figures 2-31 and 2-32 illustrate this.

To get back the original icon, Get Info on the file again. Select the icon in the Get Info window, then select **Clear** from the Edit Menu. *Presto change-o!*

To change the picture in the Puzzle desk accessory, you follow similar steps. First copy the picture you want to the clipboard

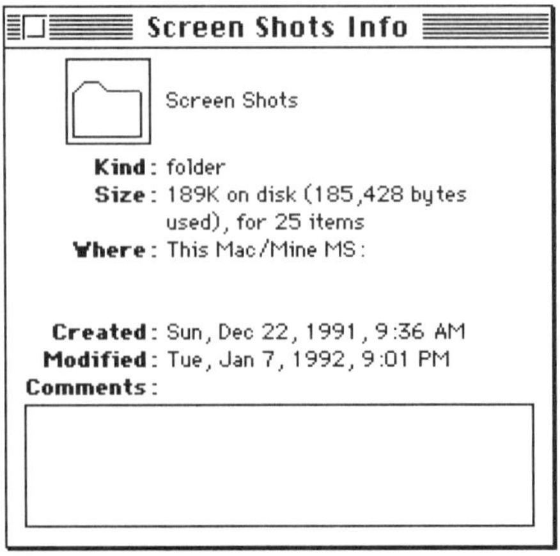

Figure 2-31. Get Info Box with the Original Icon

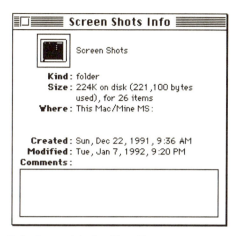

Figure 2-32. Get Info Box with the New Icon

(keep it small—about 32 by 32 pixels). Open **Puzzle DA** by selecting it from the menu. When it's open, select **Paste** from
the Edit Menu. *Et voilà!* A brand new puzzle to figure out.

Wrapping up System 7

There you have the customizing features of System 7. Some for
touch, some for sight, some for sound. They give you the flexibility
to make your Mac your own, but not so much that your Mac is
completely unique. That's where the *This Mac Is Mine* disk comes in.

Now we come to the juicy part, making your Mac one of a
kind. Be sure to read and follow the installation instructions carefully. Also read the directions for using each program *before* you
try it (I know that goes against the grain of most Mac users).
Nothing included here will physically injure your Macintosh, but
improper use could cause some nasty crashes that I'm sure you'd
rather avoid.

Startup Screens

In which Heathcliff returns from the moors with an ancient Druid scroll that reveals the secrets of replacing the "Welcome to Macintosh" screen with something a little more exciting. Catherine swoons.

This Mac Is Mine: The Startup Screen

The startup screen is a nice idea, a friendly greeting when you power up your Mac. However, after a week's worth of **Welcome to Macintosh!** you just stop seeing it. Variety is, after all, the spice of life.

Wouldn't it be nice if you could change that tired screen to suit your mood or just to welcome you personally? Well, you can. This chapter provides hints and tips on creating your own customized startup screens in your favorite drawing or painting program. We'll also use GIFConverter to convert photo-quality images into a startup screen. The startup screen in Figure 3-1 was drawn in MacPaint which, like many painting and drawing programs, gives you the option of saving your painting in startup screen format.

The screen in Figure 3-1 is simple: four boxes, some text, and two graphics copied from HyperCard's Art Bits stack. It's a small startup screen so it can be used on closed-architecture Macs like the Classic and the 512 K Mac that have small, built-in screens. Of course, it can also be used on Macs with larger monitors; it just won't fill the screen.

You'll find it on the disk as a document called StartupScreen in the PictureFiles folder. To use it, just pop it in your System Folder and restart your Mac.

Figure 3-1. *This Mac Is Mine* StartupScreen

If you already have a custom startup screen in your System Folder, you'll have to rename the old one. Call it something to remind you of its content. As in any other folder, you can't have two files with the same name, and only the one called StartupScreen will appear when you restart your Mac.

Altering the Startup Screen

There are two versions of the screen on the *This Mac Is Mine* disk. The first is called StartupScreen, and the second is called StartupScreen.Paint. It is identical to the screen in Figure 3-1, except it's in MacPaint format so you can take it apart and see how it ticks.

To customize it, just open the file with the extension .Paint into MacPaint, or any painting or drawing program that will import a MacPaint file (there are many that will). Then have fun. Add color (if your Mac and paint program are both color capable), add your name, a different greeting, or change the graphics.

Go hog-wild if you want. Trash this screen and design your own from scratch.

The important thing to remember when you create a startup screen in a paint program is that your design has to be saved in startup screen format or else it won't work. If your drawing or painting program isn't capable of saving a startup screen, don't worry. Kevin Mitchell's **GIFConverter** can do it for you. More about that later on.

A Word about Size

When you create a startup screen, whether from a paint file or a scanned photograph, bear in mind that it can't be larger than your screen or parts will get cut off at startup.

I could give you the pixel dimensions of all the Macintosh monitors available (for example, the Apple RGB 12-inch monitor has an active video display area of 205 mm by 153 mm, with a resolution of 512 horizontal pixels by 384 vertical) but I won't. First, it's as boring as tax tables. Second, all of that good information is listed in the back of your Mac or monitor manual under Specifications if you really have to know.

Instead of a bunch of dull, dry dimensions, a simple rule of thumb should do: *If you can't see the whole startup screen while you're creating it, you won't be able to see the whole screen when you use it.* Easy enough?

If, after you create a startup screen, it doesn't fill, or if it overfills your screen, go back to the program you created it in and scale it up or down. Just be warned: paint programs don't scale text very well. If you need to scale your screen more than 10 or 20 percent (in either direction), the text will probably get a bad case of jaggies. You'll get a better end product if you cut the text out before you scale, and re-enter it in an appropriate size afterward.

After you make one or two screens, you'll get a feeling for what fits on your particular monitor. All it takes is practice.

Besides, it's not the size of your screen that counts, but what you do with it.

Picture-Perfect Startup Screens with GIFConverter

If your drawing or painting program can't save your work as a startup screen, then you need GIFConverter.

GIFConverter, by Kevin Mitchell (shareware, $40) is the Swiss Army knife of graphics utilities. It's a stand-alone application that can open nine different graphics formats including GIF, PICT, startup screen, and paint files, and turn them into any of the other eight formats. It allows you to dither images, scale, crop, change their color palette, and a whole lot more.

In terms of customizing your Mac, GIFConverter is more program than you need.

Of all its great features, I'll discuss here only converting paint files and photographic quality images into startup screens. We'll barely scratch GIFConverter's surface. Once you've had your fill of making startup screens, play around with GIFConverter's other features.

You'll be amazed at what you can do to an image with an inexpensive shareware program—especially if you've ever considered shelling out $500 (or more) for a commercial program like Adobe's Photoshop or Aldus's Digital Darkroom.

GIFConverter Step by Step

Since GIFConverter is a stand-alone program, all you have to do is double-click its icon and you're off and running. You'll find it in the GIFConverter folder in the Mac/Mine Apps folder on your hard drive.

When you start up the program, you're presented with two splash screens. The first has the typical copyright information and disappears after a moment. The second is the GIFConverter registration screen.

Until you register your copy of the program with the author (by paying your shareware fee) you have to deal with the screen in Figure 3-2. When you register, you get an upgrade to the latest version of the program, a printed manual, and a software key to disable this screen. Then you never have to face it again.

Clicking on the **Print Order Form...** button will print out a copy of the registration form. Clicking on **OK** puts you in the program.

You open the graphic file you want to convert by selecting **Open** from the File menu shown in Figure 3-3, or pressing Command-O. You are presented with a standard dialog box that lets you select the disk, folder, and graphic file you want to open.

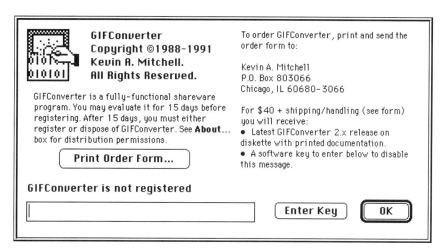

Figure 3-2. GIFConverter Registration Splash Screen

Figure 3-3. GIFConverter File Menu

The steps that follow are the same for converting paint or draw files, as well as photo-quality GIFs to startup screen format. Let's say you want to convert the file StartupScreen.Paint from the Picture Files folder, in the Mac/Mine Apps folder on your hard drive, into a functional startup screen.

GIFConverter has three search modes to look for graphic files it can open. You select them by clicking on the appropriate radio button beneath the file display. (See Figure 3-4.)

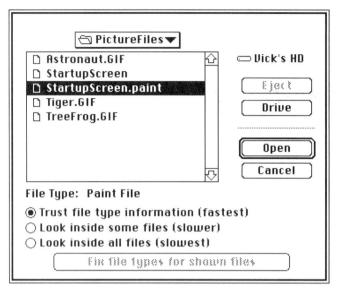

Figure 3-4. Open File Dialog

The default mode is **Trust file type information (fastest)**. The file type is the information coded into every file that tells your Mac if it's text, graphics, or an application, and what program created it.

If the graphic you want to load appears in the file display, double-clicking on its name opens the file. The StartupScreen.Paint file will appear, since GIFConverter easily reads MacPaint files.

For future reference: if a graphic file doesn't show up, it may have inaccurate file type information in its header. Try clicking on the radio button for **Look inside some files (slower)**. This setting ignores the file-type information and peeks inside some files to see if they contain information GIFConverter can use.

If the file still doesn't show up, click on the **Look inside all files (slowest)** button. Unless you've got a file format GIFConverter doesn't recognize or you're importing a PC graphic, your file should show up now.

When you get the file to appear in the file window, clicking on the **Fix file types for shown files** button will repair the file type header so you won't have to search for the fixed files ever again.

Once you've located the name of the file you want to open, you can either double-click on its name or highlight its name and click on the **Open** button. GIFConverter jumps into action.

GIFConverter opens the StartupScreen.Paint file in a standard window that can be resized like any other Mac window. If the graphic is still too large to be displayed all at once, use the horizontal and vertical scrollbars to see the rest of it. (See Figure 3-5.)

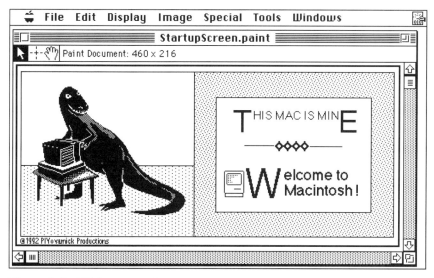

Figure 3-5. GIFConverter Screen

Since, for this example, we're only saving a paint file as a startup screen file, all we need to do is select **Save As...** from the File menu. You'll be presented with a Save dialog box.

The Save As... dialog, shown in Figure 3-6, allows you to save a copy of the currently open file in a format and location different from those of the original. The only thing GIFConverter does differently from most other programs is that it automatically adds extensions to your filename. It adds Color or Gray (often inappropriately) and then the appropriate file-type extension (like Paint or GIF).

If you work quickly, the added extensions can keep you from overwriting your original file, which is a good thing.

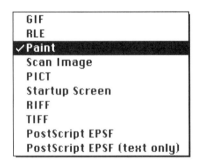

Figure 3-6. GIFConverter Save Dialog

If you're a more cautious type, you'll probably want to edit the added extension out of the name before you save. Be sure, if you edit out the added extensions, that you change the filename so it's different from the original. GIFConverter will ask before it overwrites a file, but it's best to play it safe.

To finish converting our paint file to a startup screen, click on the pop-up menu to the right of **File Type:** to get at the Save As... file format options, shown in Figure 3-7.

```
GIF
RLE
✓Paint
Scan Image
PICT
Startup Screen
RIFF
TIFF
PostScript EPSF
PostScript EPSF (text only)
```

Figure 3-7. Save As... Options

Select **Startup Screen** as the new file type. Edit the name, if you wish, then click on **Save** or press Return.

If you're an old Mac hand, you saved yourself some steps by saving the new version of your file with the name StartupScreen and having GIFConverter place it directly into your System Folder (by selecting the System Folder as the destination and changing the filename to StartupScreen before clicking on the **Save** button). You're ready to restart your Mac and try your new screen on for size.

If you didn't know you could save those steps, you have to quit to the Finder or click on the desktop to get to the Finder in System 7. However you get there, once you're in the Finder you have to drag the new screen into your System Folder. Be sure it's named StartupScreen (without spaces). If you already have a custom startup screen, or have already installed the dinosaur startup screen from the *This Mac Is Mine* disk, the system will prompt you with a message asking if it's OK to write over the existing copy. If you don't mind losing the existing screen, click on **Replace**. If you *do* mind losing it, click on the **Cancel** button and rename the existing screen before you copy your new StartupScreen file to your System Folder. Then restart.

The steps described above apply to converting any of the graphic formats GIFConverter opens into a startup screen.

For that matter, they apply to changing any one of the nine graphic formats GIFConverter reads, into any other one. Instead of startup screen format, just select the **Save As...** file type you want.

GIFConverter really expands your graphics options. No longer are you limited to the one or two formats your desktop publishing program can handle. As long as GIFConverter can read the original format and write the format your program requires, you can use the graphic. No more passing up clearance sales on clipart just because you can't use the format.

Just so you have something else to play around with, there are a few more graphic files in the PictureFiles folder on the *This Mac Is Mine* disk.

These additional pictures are photo-quality GIFs. The GIF (Graphic Interchange Format) was developed by CompuServe as a standard to simplify importing graphics files between computer platforms. Like most multiplatform "standards," GIFs aren't completely compatible between systems. You can't open some IBM GIFs on a Macintosh and vice versa.

Seems to me, what the computer industry needs is a *standard* standard, with none of this proprietary nonsense that keeps these so-called standards from being…well, standard. If nothing else, the industry CEOs should have the guts to say Macintosh standard or DOS standard, instead of getting folk's hopes up for a true multiplatform standard.

The point is that, since I am giving GIFConverter short shrift in terms of space versus capabilities, these additional graphic files are playthings you can use to explore its other functions. Check out what you can do under the Image menu if you want to have some real fun.

Some Startup Screen Design Tips

Don't get trapped. The centered, rectangular startup screen (like the one that's built into Mac system software) and full-screen photographs aren't your only options. With a paint or draw program and GIFConverter, if you can design it, you can use it as a startup screen. Let your imagination run wild.

Start with a box. Flip to the Specifications section of your monitor manual and, in your paint program, draw a box the same dimensions of (or a little smaller than) your active video display.

If your drawing program has a Show Specifications option, you can simply draw a box of any size, and change the specifications to the exact size you want (like 205 mm by 153 mm for an Apple 12-inch RGB monitor).

That's the area you have to work with.

Play with space. Instead of going with a full screen photograph (that can take up huge amounts of memory), try converting a small picture to paint format (or PICT, or whatever format your paint program imports easily) and use that as an element of your screen. Add some text if you like, and color if your Mac is able.

Break some rules. Don't worry about the rules of design (no trapped white space, balance, tension, and the like). Rules were made to be broken, right? If we were all that rigid, we'd own IBM machines. You're aiming to please yourself, not win a design competition. If you can please yourself *and* win a design competition, more power to you.

46

One rule you have to remember, though, is that you can't have more than one file in a folder with the same name. If you plan to store several startup screens in your System Folder so you can change them easily, remember to rename them. I name all my inactive screens something that suggests their contents: Penguin Scrn, or Psycho Scrn. That way, I don't have to keep opening and closing screens until I find the one I want to activate. To change screens, first rename the current Startup Screen, and then change the name of the new screen to StartupScreen. The next time you start up, the new screen will come up.

To help you get some ideas of your own, I've included a couple of possible screens in Figures 3-8 and 3-9. They aren't on the disk, just here in the text, to illustrate these simple design tips.

Figure 3-8. Psycho Sample Screen (With apologies to Janet Leigh, Alfred Hitchcock, Universal Pictures, and anyone else associated with the original *Psycho*.)

Figure 3-9. Penguin Sample Screen

Both were drawn with Symantec's GreatWorks version 2.0 using the draw and paint modules. The photograph of Janet Leigh (in Figure 3-8) was converted from GIF to PICT format using GIFConverter, following the steps outlined earlier. The penguin in Figure 3-9 was copied and pasted from HyperCard's Art Bits stack.

The final screens were saved in PICT format and converted to startup screen format, also using GIFConverter.

With any luck, these screens will provide the inspiration for you to gather your own artistic resources and design some knockout startup screens.

Just when you thought you were finished with the whole startup process, next we'll use Riccardo Ettore's StartupSndInit (that's Startup Sound INIT for the contraction-impaired) to add an audio greeting to your Mac's startup.

Chapter Four

Sound Off!

In which the quiet stranger at the boarding house magically alters the landlady's Macintosh so it says "Klaatu barrat nicto" at startup. It spouts other alien-sounding phrases at other times.

Startup Sound with StartupSndInit and Sound Mover

StartupSndInit 1.4 is part of the Sound Manager Package (Shareware, $28) written by Belgian Riccardo Ettore. The complete package includes StartupSndInit 1.4, Sound Mover 1.74, IBeep2, and SndControl.

Your shareware fee (actually 900 Belgian francs—so it could be a little more or less than $28, depending on the current exchange rate) gets you all the programs, a printed manual, and two (count 'em, *two*) 800K disks of public domain sounds. Mr. Ettore even accepts credit card payments, which speed your disks and manual to you and makes your credit card company think you're well traveled.

StartupSndInit is an INIT (or extension, in System 7 lingo) that loads at startup and plays the sound or sounds you put in it. When my Mac starts, I hear John Cleese (of "Fawlty Towers" and Monty Python fame) saying, "Hello! How very nice to see you!" You, of course, can make yours say anything you like.

How to Use StartupSndInit

StartupSndInit is like an empty disk. Unless you put something in it, it won't do anything. The first thing to do is fill it with sound. To do that, you need Sound Mover.

Sound Mover is a stand-alone utility very much like Apple's Font/DA Mover, except it handles sounds. To start it, you can either double-click on the Sound Mover icon, or double-click on the sound suitcase.

If you double-click on the Sound Mover icon, the sounds in your System file are automatically opened. If you double-click on the sound suitcase in the Sound Manager folder, Sound Mover automatically opens with those sounds.

For the sake of this walk-through, start by double-clicking on the sound suitcase in the Sound Manager folder in the Mac/Mine Apps folder on your hard drive.

Figure 4-1 shows the Sound Mover screen with the sound suitcase open in the window on the left side of your screen. Your next step is to open StartupSndInit in the window on the right-hand side. Click on the **Open...** button below that window. You'll be presented with a standard Open File dialog box, shown in Figure 4-2.

Since Sound Mover was opened from the Sound Manager folder, that folder is the one displayed in the Open File dialog. And, since StartupSndInit is also in that folder, all you have to do is

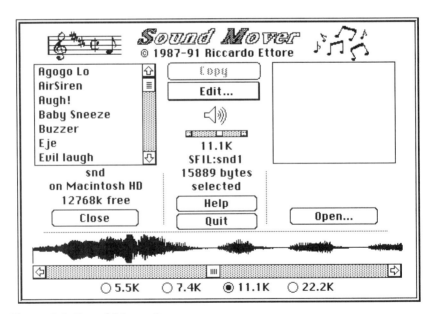

Figure 4-1. Sound Mover Screen

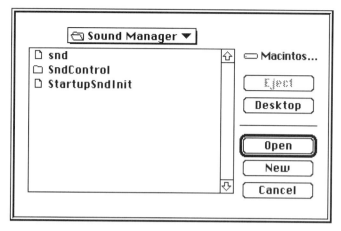

Figure 4-2. Sound Mover Open File Dialog

double-click on its name and Sound Mover opens it in the window on the right side of your screen (shown in Figure 4-3). You're ready to move sounds.

Notice that below the right-hand window, StartupSndInit's name is displayed as the currently open file. The window is empty, because the INIT contains no sound.

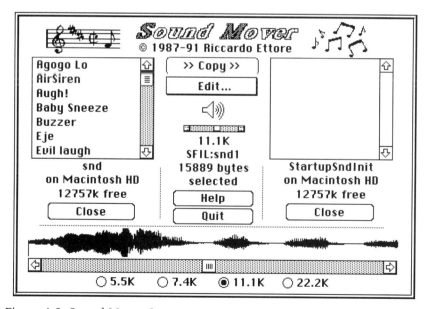

Figure 4-3. Sound Mover Screen

Listen Up!

Clicking on a sound name in the window plays that sound. Take a minute and listen to each sound in the sound suitcase.

When you decide which sound you'd like StartupSndInit to play when you power up your Mac, click on it. The >>Copy>> button becomes active. To move the selected file into StartupSndInit, just click on the >>**Copy**>> button, and a copy of the sound appears in the StartupSndInit window.

If you want to have more than one sound play at startup, just copy the additional sounds into StartupSndInit. The sounds will play sequentially in alphabetical order when the INIT loads.

If you want them to play in another order, you'll have to re-name them. Use the **Rename** option in Sound Mover's **Edit** menu. The easiest way to change their loading order is by making "A" the first letter of the sound you want to play first. Add a "B" to the second, "C" to the third, and so on.

Sounds From Anywhere

Of course, you aren't limited to the sounds that come packed in the sound suitcase. You can use Sound Mover to copy any sound file into StartupSndInit.

To get sounds from another source, click on the **Close** button under the left window, where the sound suitcase files are currently displayed. The window will clear, and the Close button changes to Open.

Click on the **Open** button. You are presented with the Open File dialog again. From here, you can navigate to any disk or folder that contains sounds.

If you already have custom sounds installed in your System file (as described in Chapter Two), you can use Sound Mover to open your custom sounds and copy one or more of them into StatupSndInit.

After loading StartupSndInit with sound, click on the **Close** button below each window. That closes both the sound suitcase and StartupSndInit. Then click on **Quit**, and you're ready to in-stall the INIT into your system.

No Tools Required

Installing this or any INIT is simple. If you're running System 6.0.X or an earlier version, just drag StartupSndInit into your System Folder. When you restart your Mac, your sound will play when the INIT loads.

If you're running System 7, you have two installation choices. The simplest is to drag the StartupSndInit icon onto your *closed* System Folder. System 7 will prompt you with the message: "Extensions need to be placed in the Extensions folder... OK?" Click on **OK**; System 7 places the INIT in the Extensions folder where it belongs. When you restart your Mac, your sound will play when the INIT loads.

If your System Folder is already open, you can drag the StartupSndInit icon directly into the Extensions folder. Restart your Mac, and your sound will play when the INIT loads.

If you want to change the order in which your INITs load (to have StartupSndInit load first, for example), read the INIT Management 101 section in Chapter Twelve.

Tips for Using StartupSndInit

In order for StartupSndInit to play a sound, your Mac's speaker volume has to be turned up to at least level 1.

If you plan to install a lot of INITs or control panel devices in one sitting —anything that requires you to restart your Mac after installation—you might want to disable StartupSndInit. Just turn your Mac's speaker volume down to level 0 before you restart. You can also drag the INIT out of your System Folder where it will quietly mind its own business until you reinstall it and restart your Mac.

Here a Sound, There a Sound, with SndControl 1.1.X

Right now, when I make a mistake on my Mac, Pee Wee Herman says, "Duh!" Actually, it's more like *"DuUUuhhh!"* It makes me feel oh-so intelligent when I screw up.

When I copy a disk—actually, when the Mac asks for a disk—Rob Schneider, from "Saturday Night Live," says, "Makin' cop-ies."

Throw something in my Mac's trash, and John Cleese says, "It's in the bin."

Some folks give me funny looks when my Mac talks. That's okay. I know it's just jealousy.

But before you get your hopes up:

- Yes, you will be able to assign your own sounds to these and other operations on your own Mac. SndControl lets you assign sounds to 13 different Finder functions.

- No, you won't be able to add these particular sounds to your Mac unless you track them down for yourself or record them yourself. The odd state of copyright laws and sound sampling makes including a famous voice on disk too risky for the lawsuit-shy.

For now, we'll use the sounds included in the Snd Suitcase in the Sound Manager folder of the *This Mac Is Mine* disk.

To record and use your very own celebrity sounds (and earn your very own celebrity lawsuits) check the Grow Your Own Sounds section of Chapter Two.

Moving On

SndControl is the third major part of the the Sound Manager package by Riccardo Ettore. It's a CDEV or control panel device that overrides the sound-playing ability of the system's Sound Control Panel. Microphone–equipped Macs, however, can still use the system's Sound Control Panel to record sounds.

There are three versions of SndControl on the *This Mac Is Mine* disk. SndControl version 1.1.1 is for System versions 6.0.4 through 6.0.7. Version 1.1.3 is for System 7. If you're running a System version earlier than 6.0.4, you'll have to use IBeep2.

IBeep2 is an early version of SndControl that functions essentially the same way later versions do, but has fewer features.

To install SndControl under either System 6.0.X or System 7, drag the appropriate SndControl icon on top of your System Folder icon. With System 6, that's all you have to do, except restart your Mac. In System 7, you'll be prompted with the message: "Control Panels need to be stored in the Control Panels folder...." Since

you'll want SndControl in that folder, click on the **OK** button, and
System 7 will finish copying the file. Restart your Mac, and you're
ready to go.

When you've opened the SndControl Control Panel (by selecting **Control Panel(s)** from the menu, then clicking (or double-
clicking for System 7) on the SndControl icon), you'll see that its
operation is fairly straightforward (Figure 4-4).

Figure 4-4. SndControl Control Panel

You select an action (like the alert Beep or Disk Eject), select a
sound to accompany it, and set the volume you want the sound
to play at.

Selecting the action is as simple as clicking on the radio button
beside its name.

To select the sound, click on its name in the scroll box. When
you select a sound, SndControl plays it for you. If you don't want
to have a sound play for a certain action, or if you want to deactivate an action–sound combination, click on the radio button beside the action and then select the blank line at the top of the
sounds list.

To set the volume, just click on the volume slide and move it to
the setting you desire. Each action–sound combination can have
a different volume setting.

Everywhere a Sound–Sound

SndControl lets you choose sounds only from those installed in your System file—not the *folder*, the actual System *file*. In System 6.0.X, its icon is a small Macintosh. In System 7, it's a suitcase.

If you have sounds scattered throughout your hard drive—and you do if you have games or applications that have their own sounds—you can use those sounds with SndControl only if you install copies of them in your System file. Sound Mover makes it easy.

System 6.0.X

To install additional sounds in your System file, you have to use Sound Mover as described in the previous section.

Start Sound Mover by double-clicking on its icon, which will automatically open the sounds in your System file. Then, in the right-hand window, open the file containing the sounds you want to copy. Navigate to your sound source the way you would to any other file or folder.

Holding down the Option key before you click on **Open**, changes it to Open Any. It gives you the option of opening any sound-file type that Sound Mover can handle. Don't be fooled, though. Sound Mover can and will open any folder or file in search of sounds, even if there are no sounds it can use in the folder. If you navigate to the heart of a file (until the Open button dims) and the file listing is blank, there aren't any sounds that Sound Mover can use. Back out of that program and try opening another. Sooner or later you'll find sounds you can use.

After you've got your sound source opened, select the sound(s) you want to move into your System file, and click on the <<**Copy**<< button.

When you're done, click on **Close** beneath each file window and quit Sound Mover. Your sounds are installed in the System file.

System 7

Installing sounds under System 7 is a little different. You can use Sound Mover with System 7; just follow the steps outlined above for System 6.0.X. If you have Sound Mover installed on your hard drive, whenever you double-click a sound suitcase you'll automatically open Sound Mover. As long as it's there, you may as well use it, but you don't have to.

If you don't have Sound Mover installed on your hard drive, you can move sounds into the System file without any special assistance. To begin, locate the sounds you want to copy to your System file. If they are stored in a suitcase, double-click on it to open it.

Select the sound or sounds you want to copy. Holding down the Option key, drag the selected items onto the System Folder icon. Holding down the Option key copies the files without moving the originals.

When you release the files, System 7 will prompt you with the message: "Sound files need to be stored in the System file...." Click on **OK**; System 7 will finish copying the files. Your sounds are added to the System file.

Tips for Using SndControl

As I mentioned in Chapter Two, if you use your Mac in a shared space—an office, living room, bedroom, or anywhere someone else is trying to work or sleep—show some consideration and turn the volume down to a comfortable level.

If you plan to change the configuration of SndControl often, be forewarned that sound files can take up lots of disk space. You may want to keep disks of sounds to store the ones you aren't currently using, rather than filling up your hard drive with megabyte after megabyte of idle sounds.

If you prefer keeping all of your sounds on your hard drive, you may want to keep ones you aren't using in a separate folder or suitcase. You can save disk space by using a compression utility like Bill Goodman's Compact Pro, a shareware program available on many electronic bulletin boards. It saves space by compressing files 50 percent or more. When you need to get at those files, Compact Pro decompresses them.

There are commercial products that compress and decompress files transparently (without you having to do anything), if you regularly need access to compressed files. Disk Doubler, from Salient Software, is one of many commercial compression products.

As hard drive real estate becomes more and more restricted—from squirreling away sounds, graphics files, or just a lot of software—a compression utility is a good idea. It has the added advantage of being cheaper than a new, larger hard drive.

Minimize to the Maximum

In which Dr. Freud says, "Some things are more useful tiny." He demon-strates this by shrinking all the open windows down to icon-size on his Mac's desktop. Anna Freud gets jealous when she sees this.

PC Envy

I used to say that I *never* get jealous of MS-DOS users; C:> prompts give me a headache. Then IBM-type software started to get GUI (for Graphical User Interface, pronounced "gooey"): as in Microsoft Windows (*ack*), O/S 2, and GEOWorks Ensemble.

I'd pooh-pooh attempts to imitate the Mac's interface, saying smart-ass things like, "If you really wanted a Macintosh, why didn't you just get one in the first place?"

Then I laid eyes on GEOWorks Ensemble—actually tried it out. It provides a very nice environment, runs on just about any MS-DOS machine (even machines that Windows sneers at, like the lowly AT), and it does something that the Mac doesn't. With Ensemble, you can minimize windows (all together now: *ooooh*).

Now I have to say I *rarely* get jealous of MS-DOS users.

Just by clicking on a button in the window's title bar, you re-duce the window (any window) to an icon that tucks itself neatly out of the way at the bottom of the screen. You can click-drag them around and put them anywhere you like. For someone like me, who has to have lots and lots of windows open all the time, it was a religious experience.

It's just too cool.

But the jealousy is gone. Thanks to Alexander Colwell's freeware INIT/control panel AltWDEF, now you can minimize windows on a Mac, too.

AltWDEF, for the contraction impaired, stands for Alternate Window Definition. It replaces the Mac's standard window definition with a non-standard (dare I say "minimalist") design.

In addition to allowing you to minimize windows, it allows you to specify the typeface and point size used for window titles, and it lets you set title justification (either right, left, or center justified) in the window's title bar.

Installing AltWDEF

There are two versions of AltWDEF in the AltWDEF folder in the Mac/Mine Apps folder on your hard drive. Version 1.6 is the current release. Version 1.4.5 is in there in case you have trouble using version 1.6 with some of your favorite applications (there are extensive notes on software incompatibilities, bugs, and so on in the AAAReadMe Teach Text file, also in the AltWDEF folder). Start with version 1.6, since it's the latest, greatest version.

Because AltWDEF is an INIT/CDEV (or control panel) combination, just drag it on top of your closed System Folder.

System 6.0.X users, when your Mac finishes copying the file, simply restart your Mac.

System 7 users will be prompted with the message "Control Panels need to be stored in the Control Panels Folder ...Okay?" Click on the **OK** button and the System will finish copying the file. Restart your Mac.

That's all there is to it.

Using AltWDEF

When your Macintosh restarts, you'll notice the difference in windows right away. If you compare Figure 5-1 (a regular Mac window) with Figure 5-2 (an AltWDEF window) you'll see what I mean.

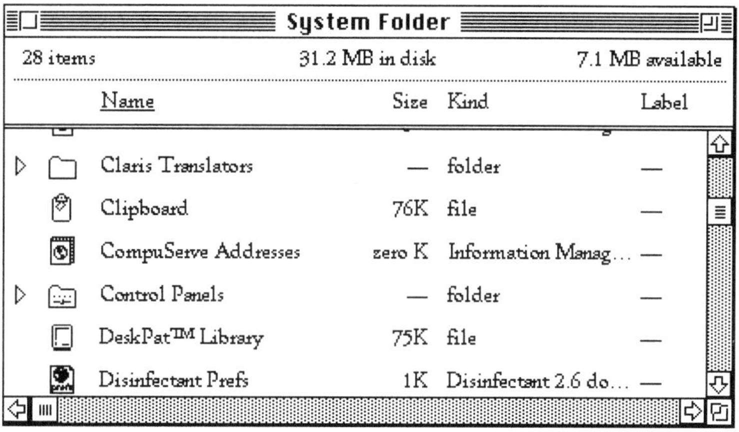

```
┌─────────────────────────────────────────────────────────────┐
│▓□▓▓▓▓▓▓▓▓▓▓▓▓ System Folder ▓▓▓▓▓▓▓▓▓▓▓▓□▓│
├─────────────────────────────────────────────────────────────┤
│  28 items          31.2 MB in disk        7.1 MB available    │
│··············································· ················· │
│         Name               Size  Kind              Label      │
├─────────────────────────────────────────────────────────────┤
│  ▷  ☐  Claris Translators    —  folder        —          ⇧   │
│     🗐  Clipboard            76K  file          —          ▤   │
│     ◉  CompuServe Addresses zero K Information Manag... —      │
│  ▷  🗀  Control Panels        —  folder        —              │
│     ☐  DeskPat™ Library     75K  file          —              │
│     🗎  Disinfectant Prefs    1K  Disinfectant 2.6 do... — ⇩  │
│⟨□ ▥ ▓▓▓▓▓▓▓▓▓▓▓▓▓▓▓▓▓▓▓▓▓▓▓▓▓▓▓▓▓▓▓▓▓▓▓▓▓▓▓ ⇨▐│
└─────────────────────────────────────────────────────────────┘
```

Figure 5-1. Standard Macintosh Window

The regular window is, well, regular. You've seen it a million times before. The AltWDEF window, on the other hand, has a snazzy new button (the minimize button) beside the old zoom button. The title is justified left, beside the close button. But that's just the beginning. You haven't even seen the AltWDEF Control Panel yet, and that's where you take control of how your windows will look.

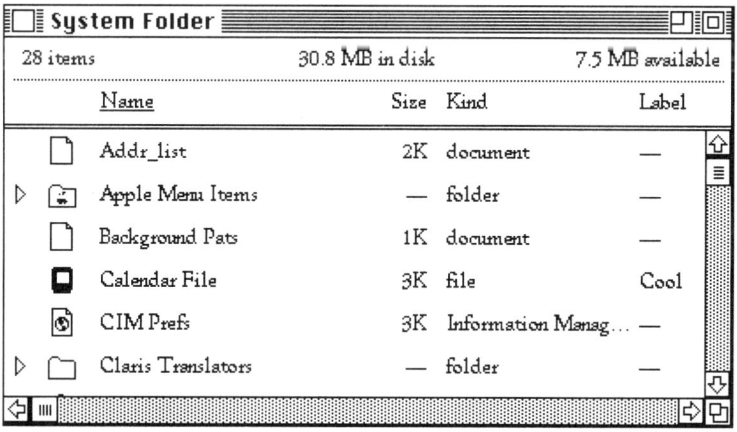

```
┌─────────────────────────────────────────────────────────────┐
│▓☐▓ System Folder ▓▓▓▓▓▓▓▓▓▓▓▓▓▓▓▓▓▓▓▓▓▓▓▓▓□▓◻│
├─────────────────────────────────────────────────────────────┤
│  28 items          30.8 MB in disk        7.5 MB available    │
│··············································· ················· │
│         Name               Size  Kind              Label      │
├─────────────────────────────────────────────────────────────┤
│     ☐  Addr_list             2K  document      —          ⇧   │
│  ▷  🗀  Apple Menu Items      —  folder        —          ▤   │
│     ☐  Background Pats        1K  document      —              │
│     ■  Calendar File          3K  file         Cool           │
│     ◉  CIM Prefs             3K  Information Manag... —        │
│  ▷  🗀  Claris Translators    —  folder        —          ⇩   │
│⟨□ ▥ ▓▓▓▓▓▓▓▓▓▓▓▓▓▓▓▓▓▓▓▓▓▓▓▓▓▓▓▓▓▓▓▓▓▓▓▓▓▓▓ ⇨▐│
└─────────────────────────────────────────────────────────────┘
```

Figure 5-2. AltWDEF Window

61

The AltWDEF Control Panel

Open the AltWDEF Control Panel by the method appropriate to your version of the System software. You'll see the control panel shown in Figure 5-3. In order of appearance the controls are: the Enabled check box, Font/Size Attributes menus, Title Bar Attributes, Miscellaneous Attributes, and the Show ICON at startup check box.

Figure 5-3. AltWDEF Control Panel

Clicking on the **?** button, by the way, brings up information about the program's author. If you like his CDEV, why not drop him a note?

Enabled Check Box

The Enabled check box lets you turn AltWDEF on and off. When the box is checked, AltWDEF is turned on.

You can toggle AltWDEF on and off as you please, without having to restart your Mac; however, the results aren't immediate. If you're turning AltWDEF off, any windows that were open before you turned it off will retain the alternate window definition until you close and reopen them. If you're turning AltWDEF on, then any open windows will retain the standard window definition until you close and reopen them.

You'll find that's true for any other changes you make in this control panel.

Font/Size Attributes

The Font/Size Attributes pane of the control panel is where you set the font for window names, both in the regular and minimized sizes.

The Main pop-up menu (shown with Chicago selected in Figure 5-3) sets the font for the title bar of full-sized windows. Clicking on the font pop-up menu presents you with a list of all the fonts installed in your System (as shown in Figure 5-4). Beside it is the size menu, which is a pop-up menu of all the sizes available in the selected typeface (as shown in Figure 5-5).

Figure 5-4. The Font Menu

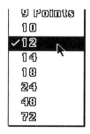

Figure 5-5. The Size Menu

You can select any available typeface and size, but selecting a size over 18 points makes your windows look ridiculous. The title bar gets huge and unwieldy. Unless you really need to, keep to smaller sizes. Also, sizes that appear in outline style (12) in the menu are the sizes that look less jagged on your screen.

The ICON option (shown with Geneva selected in Figure 5-3) sets the typeface and size for the title in the minimized, icon-sized window. The font and size menus work exactly the same as they did for the full-sized window, and the same suggestions about size also apply here.

You may change the font for full-sized and minimized windows at any time, but as with the Enabled check box, windows open at the time you make a change will not show the new font unless you close and reopen the windows.

Title Bar Attributes

The Title Bar Attributes pane of the control panel lets you set how the titles are displayed in full-sized windows. The window's title can be left, center, or right justified by clicking on the appropriate radio button.

You can also set the order in which the shrink and zoom buttons appear in the title bar. Selecting the **Shrink Order** radio button makes the buttons appear with the zoom button first, then the shrink button.

Selecting the **Zoom Order** reverses the order, putting the shrink button first, and then the zoom button (as shown in Figure 5-6). I prefer Zoom Order, because it leaves the zoom button in the same position as in a standard Macintosh window. As much as I like to tinker with my Mac, I am a creature of habit.

Figure 5-6. Title Bar with Buttons in Zoom Order

The Like Apple check box, when selected, duplicates the title bar stripe pattern from the standard window (also shown in Figure 5-6). Deselecting this option leaves you with a plain title bar (as shown in Figure 5-7).

Figure 5-7. Plain (Non-Apple) Title Bar

As before, you can change these options at any time, but windows already open when you make a change will not show the changes until you close and reopen the windows.

Misc Attributes

In the Misc Attributes pane of the control panel, you set how and where your minimized windows will line up when you shrink them. The default setting is Bottom: Left to Right (as shown back in Figure 5-3), which means the minimized windows will drop to the bottom of your screen and line up from left to right. Selecting the Shrink pop-up menu displays your other options (see Figure 5-8). If you have set a staggered icon grid with Layout (Chapter Six) or System 7's Views Control Panel, the minimized windows will fall into the staggered pattern.

Figure 5-8. The Shrink Menu

I prefer the default setting myself. Having the icons collect at the right side of my screen, either top to bottom or vice versa, gets in the way of my disk and trash icons. Try each option until you find the one that suits you—or, you can just click-drag the minimized windows and place them anywhere you like. It's a free country.

Exclude Applications

The Exclude Applications button is very handy. Not all programmers use the standard Apple window definition—Microsoft products are famous for this. For example, Microsoft Excel 2.0 simply overrides AltWDEF with its own window definition. Others may try to override it and, failing, crash your system.

Should you run into a program (application, DA, or whatever) that crashes with AltWDEF installed, you can exclude it. AltWDEF will leave the excluded applications alone. The author, Alexander Colwell, recommends excluding Microphone II and HyperCard because of a known conflict.

To exclude an application, click on the **Exclude Applications...** button. You'll be presented with the dialog shown in Figure 5-9. Using the upper scroll box, navigate to the application you want to exclude from AltWDEF. Click on the application's name, then click on the **Add** button. The application's name is added to the lower scroll box named Applications to be excluded.

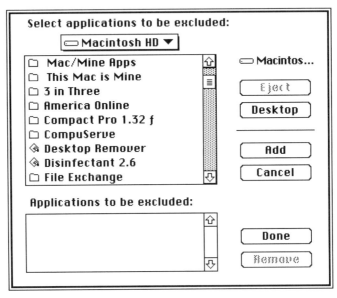

Figure 5-9. Exclude Applications Dialog

Exclude as many applications as you need or want to exclude. When you're finished, click on the **Done** button. You're done.

If, at a later date, you decide you no longer want to exclude an application, just click on its name in the Applications to be excluded scroll box and click on the **Remove** button. AltWDEF will again try to work its magic on that application.

Living with AltWDEF

Once you have AltWDEF configured the way you like, you're ready to shrink away. If you work like I do, you have a bunch of windows open on the desktop, just like you have piles of paper and whatnot scattered all over your desk. Wading through them can be a real hassle. Sometimes, for instance when you copy and paste between documents, it's a necessary evil (we'll eliminate some of the problems with copying between multiple windows with WindowShade in Chapter Ten).

But even when it isn't practical, I usually have quite a few windows open. Eventually I wind up calling each window to the front to remind myself of what I'm doing. With AltWDEF, I can shrink the windows down to icon size along the bottom of my monitor (as shown in Figure 5-10) just by clicking on the shrink button. The name of the mini-window jogs my memory enough to remind me of what's going on.

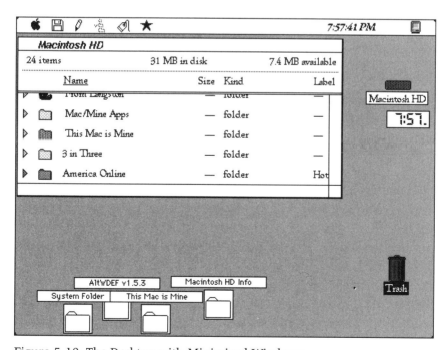

Figure 5-10. The Desktop with Minimized Windows

By the way, each minimized window icon counts as an open window to the Finder. Under System 6.0.X, you can have a maximum of fourteen windows open at once; however, you can up the ante and set a higher maximum with Layout (see Chapter Six).

When you need to refer to a window's contents, simply click on the shrink button again (or the right side of the mini-title bar, if the icon isn't selected), and the window springs back to full size. Sometimes I get so carried away, I feel like Dr. Cyclops (from the B-movie of the same name), shrinking and unshrinking every window in sight

Yes. I *am* a toy brain.

If your Mac desktop is as cluttered as the top of your desk, you'll find AltWDEF's minimized windows a great organizing tool—it's almost like having In and Out baskets for your desktop. You could use the lower right side of your monitor for minimized "To-do" windows, the left for "Done" or tickler files—whatever suits your style.

Even if you don't need help organizing your life (yeah, right), you'll find the ability to shrink and unshrink your windows totally cool.

Get Organized with Layout

*In which Bartleby, in a fit of pique, reorganizes the System 6.0.X Finder
so it does exactly what he wants. Shortly after, he is committed.*

System 6.0.X users, are you tired of hearing about the mondo
cool things that System 7 lets you do? Ready to bash in the brains
of the next byte-head who smugly disparages your dirty ROMs?
Don't get mad—get even.

With **Layout** 1.9 you can have at least one of the options
System 7 users are crowing about—without having to spend a
bazillion dollars on RAM and software upgrades. Layout gives
you many of the features of System 7's Views control panel plus
some features Views doesn't have.

Layout 1.9, a public domain (free!) application by Michael C.
O'Connor, lets you reconfigure your file and folder display almost any way you like. Layout not only lets you specify the
typeface and size used for file and folder names, it also lets you
customize the amount of space between files and folders and
specify how much the files and folders are offset in a staggered
layout. System 7 just lets you choose between staggered or straight
fixed grids.

Layout à la Carte

Layout is a complex application. That doesn't mean it's difficult
to use—far from it—it just means it does an awful lot. Rather
than confuse the issue by jumping around from menu to menu,

option to option, doing a sample Finder reconfiguration, let's walk through Layout's menus.

I'll cover each menu individually, saying a little about what each menu option does. As you read, follow along using Layout on your own Mac. While you do, think about how you use your Mac and how you might use Layout to customize your own Finder. Later you can pick and choose your own Finder changes from these command summaries.

Start Your Engines

Since Layout is a stand-alone application, start by double-clicking on its icon. You'll find it in the System 6.0.X Only folder of the Mac/Mine Apps folder on your hard drive.

When Layout starts, it looks for the Finder in your current System Folder. If you are running MultiFinder or if Layout can't locate the Finder, you're prompted with the screen shown in Figure 6-1. It allows you either to quit Layout so you can deactivate MultiFinder (under which the Finder is *always* in use, and therefore cannot be altered) or to choose another Finder to customize.

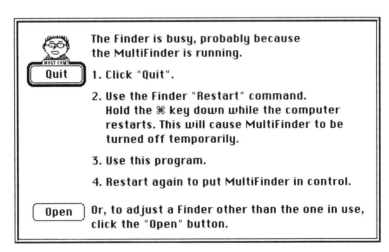

Figure 6-1. Finder is Busy Dialog

If you're running MultiFinder and want to adjust your current Finder, you need to deactivate MultiFinder. Click on the **Quit** button. Restart your Mac while holding down the Command key to deactivate MultiFinder. You can now use Layout to adjust the Finder.

If you aren't running MultiFinder and Layout still can't locate your Finder, click on the **Open** button. You are presented with a standard Open File dialog. Use it to navigate to the Finder you want to customize and open it.

When Layout has the open Finder, your screen will look something like the one shown in Figure 6-2. The large window simulates a Finder window, complete with dummy files. The text box at the bottom of the screen gives you brief help summaries, reminding you of what you can do in the current window. For more detailed help, go to the menu.

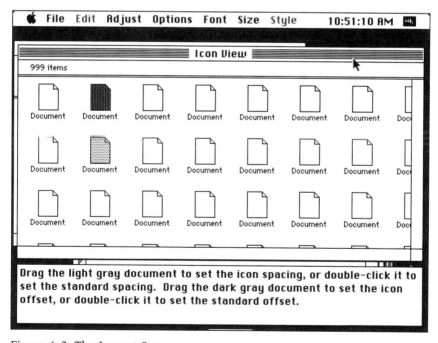

Figure 6-2. The Layout Screen

The Menu

Like all good Macintosh programs, Layout adds it own online help function to the menu. You can access it any time Layout is open. Select **About Layout** from the menu. You'll see the dialog box shown in Figure 6-3. It presents you a summary of all the commands available in Layout. Use the scroll bar at the right to read the rest of the documentation.

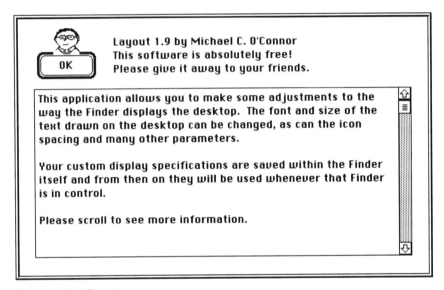

Figure 6-3. About Layout

The File Menu

Open

The File menu (see Figure 6-4) gives you your standard file opening and saving features. You use the Open command if you plan to customize more than one Finder. For example, after you finish customizing the Finder on your hard drive, you might want to customize the Finder on a rescue disk you keep handy in case of emergency.

Save

The Save command records the changes you've made to the Finder. The changes are permanent until you change them again with Layout.

Figure 6-4. The File Menu

By the Way

A rescue disk, if you don't already have one, is a good idea—especially when you're messing around with the Finder. If something horrible happens to your hard drive or if your System file gets corrupted or damaged, you can boot from your rescue disk and try to repair or salvage your hard drive's contents.

A rescue disk should have a no-frills copy of your System Folder (no extra fonts, INITs, or control panels), a copy of the Finder (in the System Folder), and a disk repair utility like Apple's **Disk First Aid**.

System 7 users might want to install an earlier version of the system on their rescue disks. Although a pared down version of System 7 will fit on a high-density floppy disk, you can't do much with it. System 7 also runs slowly from a floppy.

Revert

The Revert command, unlike the Save command, discards changes that were recently made to the Finder, restoring it to the last *saved* version. If you want to undo changes you've already saved, you have to correct them manually and save the new version.

Defaults

The Defaults command discards all changes made to the Finder, even those that have been saved. It restores all Finder settings to their defaults, which means that the Finder will look exactly as it did when you first loaded it on your Mac.

Get From

The Get From command copies your Finder settings from one Finder to another. If you want to customize the Finder on a rescue disk as we discussed above, you can select **Get From** from the File menu and copy the Layout settings from the Finder on your hard drive to the Finder on your rescue disk, without having to redo each setting manually.

Quit

The Quit command exits Layout. If you quit without saving your changes to the Finder, Layout will ask you if want to save the changes. At this prompt you can save or discard the new changes or cancel the quit and continue working with Layout. Just click the appropriate button.

The Edit Menu

The Edit menu is available only when you are running a DA with Layout. It contains the standard Undo, Cut, Copy, Paste, and Clear commands, but has no effect on either Layout or the Finder. The Edit menu is grayed out almost all the time.

The Adjust Menu

The Adjust menu (See Figure 6-5) lets you alter each of the Finder's displays. This is where Layout starts to get complex, so stay with me.

Figure 6-5. The Adjust Menu

Small Icon View

Selecting Small Icon View gives you a view of the desktop with small icons displayed beside the file names. You can adjust the spacing between files both vertically and horizontally (see Figure 6-6) by dragging the gray icon to the desired position.

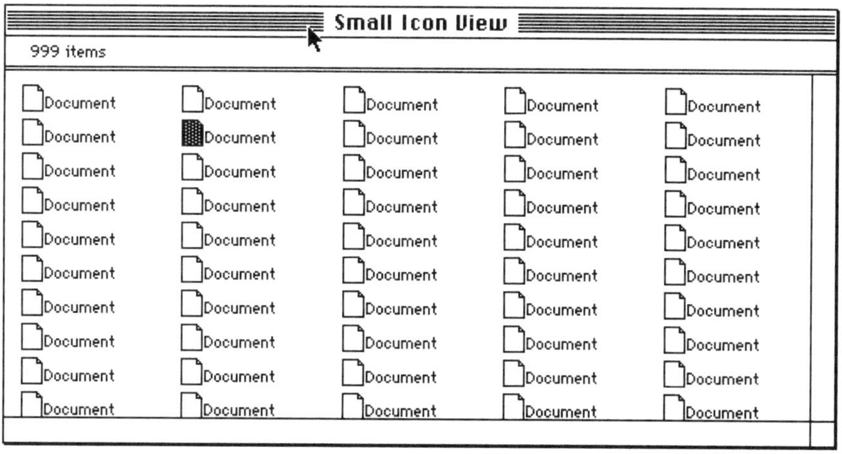

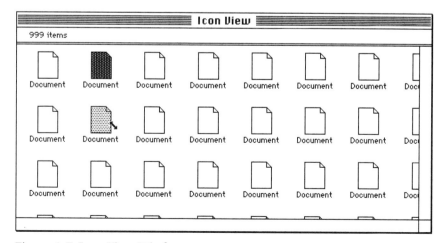

Figure 6-6. Small Icon View Window

Icon View

Icon View is Layout's default display mode. When you first opened Layout, you saw the Icon View shown in Figure 6-7. Dragging the dark gray icon lets you change the vertical grid spacing; that is, you set how much lower every alternate icon will be (as shown in Figure 6-8).

Figure 6-7. Icon View Window

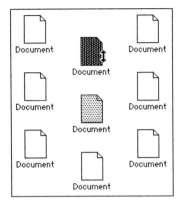

Figure 6-8. Vertical Grid Spacing

The light gray icon lets you set the horizontal offset. Once the columns are staggered vertically with the dark icon, dragging the light gray icon lets you move the columns closer together or further apart. Leave enough space between columns so your file names don't overlap icons or other file names. (see Figure 6-9).

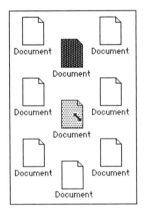

Figure 6-9. Horizontal Offset

Text Views

The Text Views option lets you alter the parameters that control the View by Name, Size, Date, and Kind display (shown in Figure 6-10). You can adjust column spacing by dragging the appropriate dotted line. Dragging a dotted line to the right enlarges the column and pushes columns to the right of it further right.

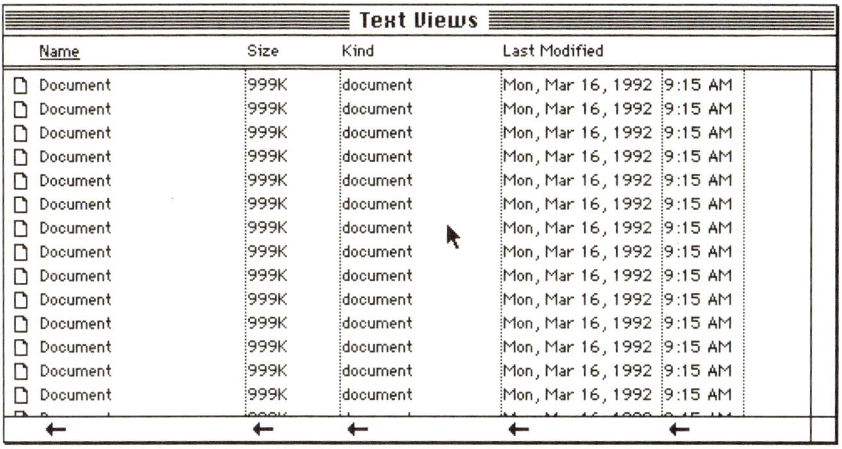

Text Views				
Name	Size	Kind	Last Modified	
🗋 Document	999K	document	Mon, Mar 16, 1992	9:15 AM
🗋 Document	999K	document	Mon, Mar 16, 1992	9:15 AM
🗋 Document	999K	document	Mon, Mar 16, 1992	9:15 AM
🗋 Document	999K	document	Mon, Mar 16, 1992	9:15 AM
🗋 Document	999K	document	Mon, Mar 16, 1992	9:15 AM
🗋 Document	999K	document	Mon, Mar 16, 1992	9:15 AM
🗋 Document	999K	document	Mon, Mar 16, 1992	9:15 AM
🗋 Document	999K	document	Mon, Mar 16, 1992	9:15 AM
🗋 Document	999K	document	Mon, Mar 16, 1992	9:15 AM
🗋 Document	999K	document	Mon, Mar 16, 1992	9:15 AM
🗋 Document	999K	document	Mon, Mar 16, 1992	9:15 AM
🗋 Document	999K	document	Mon, Mar 16, 1992	9:15 AM
🗋 Document	999K	document	Mon, Mar 16, 1992	9:15 AM
🗋 Document	999K	document	Mon, Mar 16, 1992	9:15 AM
←	←	←	←	←

Figure 6-10. Text Views Window

Dragging a dotted line to the left narrows the column and pulls columns to the right of it further left. If you narrow a column too much, the Finder cuts off any text that won't fit. Layout flags this problem by showing text overlaps where two columns collide.

In addition to changing the width of the columns, you can change the alignment of the text in each column—it can be either right or left justified. Clicking on the arrow at the base of each column toggles the direction of justification.

Double-clicking on the Date column changes the way the date is displayed. Layout will give you one of three date displays each time you double-click the Date column. In order of appearance, they are: slash notation (3/16/92); complete (Monday, March 16, 1992); or abbreviated (Mon Mar 16, 1992).

Changes made under the Text Views option affect the Finder only when it is displaying by Name, Size, Date, or Kind, not in Icon or Small Icon views.

Default Window
The Default Window (as shown in Figure 6-11) creates a window template for any new windows created by the Finder. Drag the window to the position on screen where you want all new windows to appear by click-dragging on the window's title bar. If you want your hard drive's window always to be visible, drag the

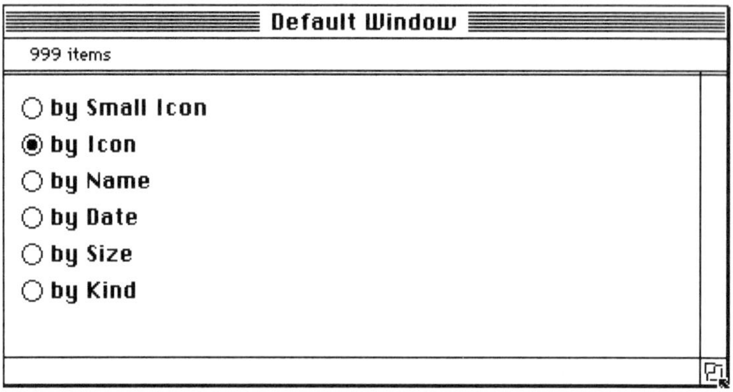

```
≡≡≡≡≡≡≡≡≡  Default Window  ≡≡≡≡≡≡
 999 items
   ○ by Small Icon
   ⦿ by Icon
   ○ by Name
   ○ by Date
   ○ by Size
   ○ by Kind
```

Figure 6-11. The Default Window

Default Window below or to one side of it. Resize the Default Window by click-dragging the size box at the window's bottom right corner.

When you click on one of the radio buttons inside the Default Window, you choose the way that a newly formatted disk's window is displayed. You can set it to view by Small Icon, Icon, Name, Date, Size, and Kind.

These buttons affect only the displays of newly formatted disks. The windows of new folders retain the view-by display of the disk or folder in which they are created.

Grid

Selecting Grid from the Adjust menu toggles on and off an invisible grid in the window. When the grid is on, adjustments you make to icon spacing in the Icon View and Small Icon View automatically snap to the invisible grid.

The Grid feature is on if a check mark appears next to its name in the Adjust menu. Reselecting Grid from the menu will deactivate it.

The Options Menu

The Options menu, shown in Figure 6-12, gives you control over a number of Finder functions that are normally beyond your control.

```
┌─────────────────────────────┐
│ Options                     │
├─────────────────────────────┤
│ ✓Use Zoom Rects             │
│  Always Grid Drags          │
│  Skip Trash Warnings        │
│  Title Bar Click            │
│  Use Physical Icon          │
│  Copy Inherit               │
│  New Folder Inherit         │
│               ▸             │
│  Watch Threshold...         │
│  Max Windows...             │
│  Color Style...             │
└─────────────────────────────┘
```

Figure 6-12. The Options Menu

Use Zoom Rects

This feature is active by default. It allows the Finder to continue to use its zooming rectangle animation whenever it opens a file, folder, or application. If you're more interested in speed than visual fireworks, deactivate this option. Turning it off will save you a few microseconds here and there.

Always Grid Drags

This menu option is inactive by default. If Always Grid Drags is active, whenever you drag and release a file or folder in a window, the file or folder snaps to the nearest grid position available. I find it annoying, you may not. Try it and see.

Skip Trash Warnings

When Skip Trash Warnings is selected, the Finder will not warn you when you throw an application or System file into the trash. The danger potential is too high. I'd leave this option turned off, but then, I'm the cautious type.

Title Bar Click

The Title Bar Click is another option that is normally inactive. If you activate it, whenever you double-click a window's title bar, its parent window (the window that displays the folder that the current window represents) will open, or come forward on the desktop if it's all ready open.

   If you intend to use WindowShade (described in Chapter Ten), I'd leave this option inactive as well.

Use Physical Icon

The Use Physical Icon option may or may not have an effect on your Macintosh. With some Mac models, activating this feature changes the desktop icons of disks and devices from an icon of their respective media (like a floppy disk), to an icon of the physical drive (like an external floppy drive). With other Macs, it won't do anything.

Try it, don't try it. Suit yourself.

If you decide to try the Physical Icon option and it works on your machine, be aware that if you want to remove the option later you'll probably have to restart your Mac afterwards.

Whenever you change icons in the Finder (or add icon replacements for menu text, as we will with MICN in Chapter Seven), icon spacing is changed. If you revert to a larger icon, it could get mangled—have parts lopped off, or be all bunched up with other icons. A simple restart should fix it, but you could also use Layout's Revert option (under the Edit menu) to restore your Finder settings to the last saved version, or the Default option to restore all of the original Finder settings. See the Edit Menu section earlier in this chapter for more information.

Copy Inherit

When the Copy Inherit option is activated, folder characteristics (like color, view type, and size) are passed on to duplicate folders when a copy is made.

New Folder Inherit

As with Copy Inherit, activating New Folder Inherit passes on a folder's characteristics (color, view type, and size) to any new folders created inside it.

Watch Threshold

The Watch Threshold option (Figure 6-13) lets you set how long the Finder waits before it turns the arrow cursor into the animated watch cursor. The watch cursor comes up in lengthy operations like disk copying and formatting. If it really matters to you, change it, otherwise, I'd just leave it alone. The Finder manages its cursors well enough on its own.

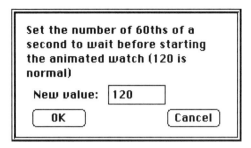

Figure 6-13. Watch Threshold Dialog

Max Windows

This option lets you set the maximum number of windows that can be open on the desktop at one time. Selecting it calls up the dialog shown in Figure 6-14. You may *want* to have hundreds of open windows, but the more you have open, the more memory the Finder uses—and the slower your system will get, since it has to redraw all those windows every time you make a change.

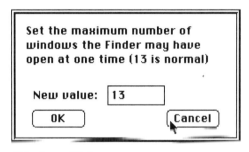

Figure 6-14. Max Windows Dialog

If you change the maximum number of windows, keep it to a realistic number. Can you really work effectively with more than eleven or twelve windows open at a time?

Color Style

If you have a color Mac and Color QuickDraw installed, the Color Style option (Figure 6-15) lets you change the way desktop icons are colored. Click on the radio button beside the icon style you prefer, either the normal outline, or the alternate filled-in version.

You can also change the eight colors under the Finder's Color menu. Click on one of the eight colors, which calls up the color

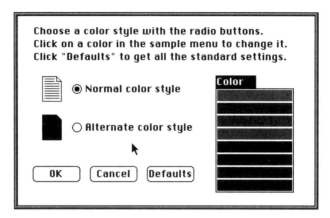

Figure 6-15. Color Style Dialog

wheel dialog we used (back in Chapter Two) to select a highlight color. You can either tweak a default color to another shade or choose a new color entirely.

The Font Menu

The Font Menu (shown in Figure 6-16) lets you change the display font for most of the text that appears in Finder windows (including icon names, the disk information displayed beneath the window's title bar, and all the text in Text Views).

Figure 6-16. The Font Menu

The Font Menu displays the names of the fonts installed in your System file. Just select the font you want to use. The change takes effect immediately.

The Size Menu

The Size menu (shown in Figure 6-17) lets you choose the size of the typeface you selected from the Font menu. You can select any available size, but those that are displayed in outline style, like 18, will have the least jagged edges on screen and be easier to read, especially in larger sizes.

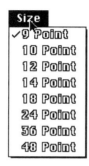

Figure 6-17. The Size Menu

The number of sizes that are displayed in outline style varies from typeface to typeface. How a typeface looks at different sizes is a result of the kind of font it is. A bitmapped font looks more jagged the larger it gets. PostScript fonts, with Adobe Type Manager installed in your system, look good at any size, as do TrueType fonts.

The Style Menu

The Style Menu (shown in Figure 6-18) is active only when the Text Views option under the Adjust menu is used. You can apply Bold, Italic, Underline, Outline, and Shadow styles to the text at the head of the column by which the view is sorted.

Figure 6-18. The Style Menu

In other words, if you select Outline under the Style menu, later, when you use View by Name in the Finder, the column heading Name will appear in outline style. If you use View by Date, then the word Date will be in outline style. It's an at-a-glance way of seeing how your files are being sorted in a text display.

Wrapping Up Layout

As you can tell from the abundance of features, Layout is a powerful tool for customizing the Finder in System 6.0.X.

The abundance of features also makes it pointless for me to try to tell you what to do with Layout. Only you know which of its features will complement how you work and which will bog you down. Let me just suggest one thing: don't use Layout right away.

Instead, while you're working and playing with your Macintosh, keep a piece of paper and a pencil handy (or use the Note Pad DA, under the  menu) and jot down the things in the Finder you'd change if you could. For the moment, limit yourself to practical things, things that will make working easier for you, or faster. There's always time to play with cosmetic changes to the Finder later.

After you've worked on your wish list for a few hours or days, compare it to Layout's capabilities. Change the things that match up.

With a little time and patience, Layout can give you the Finder of your dreams.

Menu Bar Icons with MICN

In which Mrs. Malaprop exclaims, "Icon cook too!" and reduces all of her menu bar headings to tiny icons that save space and add efficiency.

Who says it's lonely at the top? Just look at the top of your Mac's screen. Nothing is lonely in the menu bar; if anything, it's too crowded—especially if you're running System 7 with that blasted Balloon Help icon in the way all the time.

The Finder is bad enough. If you open an application like CompuServe Information Manager or an integrated package like GreatWorks, there's hardly any room left in the menu bar. Some of us have a double whammy. I've got SuperClock! installed (see Chapter Eight), which adds a clock to the menu bar. And I've got a Global Village **TelePort/Fax** modem, which, when it's in use, gives you a handy-dandy thermometer graph in the menu bar, so you can see how fast data is transferring. Sometimes I feel like the Mad Hatter at the tea party, yelling "No room! No room!" With a 12-inch monitor my menu bar is cramped and hard to read. The same menu bar on a Mac with a built-in 9-inch monitor is downright unreadable. Well, **MICN** is here to change all that.

MICN (pronounced *"My-con,"* to rhyme with icon), a public domain (free!) control panel by Mark Valence, replaces space-hogging words in the menu bar with teeny icons that take up almost no space at all.

Installing MICN

Since MICN is a CDEV, installation is simple: just drag the MICN icon (from the MICN folder in the Mac/Mine Apps folder on your hard drive) and drop it on top of your closed System Folder. With System 6.0.X that's all you have to do, except restart your Mac.

Under System 7, you will be prompted with the message, "Control Panels need to be stored in the Control Panels folder..." Click on the **OK** button, and System 7 will finish moving the file. You're ready to go—just restart your Mac.

Using MICN

After your Mac goes through its restart sequence, you'll see your System 7 menu bar has changed into the one shown in Figure 7-1. The 🍎 menu icon remains the same. The disk icon replaces the word File, the pencil replaces Edit, the three stacked file folders replace the word Views, the tag replaces Labels, and the star replaces Special. The menu functions remain exactly the same.

Figure 7-1. System 7 Menu Bar After MICN

Under System 6.0.X, a similar transformation has taken place, except MICN hasn't replaced the menu header Color with an icon. Read on to see how to select a new icon for it.

The change from words to icons may take some getting used to. In the first place, you have to remember what the new icons stand for—that isn't so bad, as the icons are fair representations of the former names. The other thing that takes getting used to is mousing around to the various menus. Since the icons take up so much less space than the words they replace, you'll find yourself selecting the wrong menu just because your muscle memory (mouse-al memory?) hasn't quite caught on to the smaller distances. That will change with time.

You can add and remove as many menu replacements as you'd like in a session. I added a replacement for the Mail and Go To menu headings in America Online. System 6.0.X users might want to add a new title to iconize the Color menu heading. None of the changes take effect until you restart your Mac, so when you are through adding to the menu menu, close the MICN Control Panel by clicking the close box. When you return to the Finder, select Restart from the Special (now a star icon) menu.

Once your Mac restarts and you are back in the Finder, open the application you added menu replacements for and see your changes. Figure 7-5 shows my new menu bar icons for America Online.

Figure 7-5. MICN-ized America Online Menu Bar

Removing MICN

If, for some reason, you want to remove MICN, rest assured the process is simple enough. First open the MICN Control Panel and click on the **Off** radio button. Close the control panel and click-drag the MICN icon out of your System Folder and into a holding folder, into the trash, or onto a disk. Restart your Mac.

It's important that you restart after removing MICN. If you don't, your menu headings all get chopped off, since MICN has only allowed each heading enough space to display the assigned icon. The word Labels will look like Lab, Menu will be cut to Men, and so on.

Getting Fancy

As is, MICN is fun, flexible, and practical, but it can do more. If you are literate with ResEdit, Apple's Resource editor for the Macintosh, you can customize MICN even further.

The MICN docs file, a TeachText file (included in the MICN folder in the Mac/Mine Apps folder on your hard drive), gives you all the technical specifications you need to create completely new icons for MICN to use. You can also create special MICN lists for individual applications with ResEdit. Instead of having to cram all the variations of menu bar headings into MICN through the menu menu, you can tailor a custom listing for each application you use.

You can also create a new icon for MICN's use right in the control panel, without resorting to ResEdit. The procedure is the same as discussed in the Shrink to Fit section of this chapter except you select the blank space at the far right end of the horizontal icon scroll, rather than an icon. You can then use the bottom windows to create an icon from scratch, rather than editing an existing icon, and press the + button to select the new icon.

Be warned, however: some folks have crashed when trying this, or it just hasn't worked. Approach with caution. While I haven't had a problem using this option on my LC with System 7 (nor has my friend Mark Carter who road tested MICN and some other programs for me on his IIsi and Mac Plus), this feature should be considered armed and potentially dangerous. If you try it and have a problem, don't say I didn't warn you.

With MICN, no matter which version of the Mac's system you use, you can reclaim about half the menu bar for other uses. System 7 users will be able to squeeze out a little more space in Chapter Eight, when we look at NoBalloonMenu.

Telling Time All the Time with SuperClock!

In which the White Rabbit, always late, installs SuperClock! in his menu bar to keep from losing his head and track of time. The Mad Hatter makes room for it in System 7 by removing the Balloon Help menu.

SuperClock! Version 3.9.1

Steve Christensen's **SuperClock!**, a freeware control panel, puts a clock right where you need it most —in the menu bar— so you can use it all the time.

Speaking for myself, I dislike the Alarm Clock DA that comes bundled with the Mac's System software. Not the clock itself, which is perfectly functional, but the fact that it's a desk accessory. Whenever I realize I need the clock, I'm usually wrapped up in something else (downloading a file from a pay-by-the-minute service) that keeps me from getting at the menu. Or else I remember to start the clock up, but all the open windows hide the desktop and I can't find it. The clock doesn't have the sense to stay up front where it's useful, but always migrates to the bottom of the window heap.

With SuperClock!, all I have to do is look at the upper right corner of my screen. If I'm online, I can use it as a stopwatch to keep track of my time and money. In comparison to the Alarm Clock DA, SuperClock! is light-years ahead.

Installing SuperClock!

Since SuperClock! is a control panel, installation is easy. Drag its icon into your System Folder (System 6.0.X) or into your Control Panels folder in your System Folder (System 7) and restart your Mac. Under System 7, you can also just drag it on top of your closed System Folder and click on **OK** when asked if it's OK to copy SuperClock! to the Control Panels folder.

When the system finishes copying the file, restart your Mac. The SuperClock! appears in your menu bar. It automatically reads your system clock for time and date, all that remains for you to do is to customize it to your liking.

Using SuperClock!

Open the SuperClock! Control Panel by the method appropriate to your version of the System software. You'll be presented with the window shown in Figure 8-1.

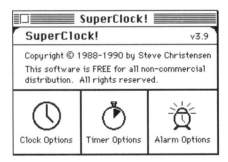

Figure 8-1: The SuperClock! Control Panel

SuperClock! gives you three sets of options: Clock, Timer, and Alarm. Clicking on the option you want to change calls up that customizing window. First set the basic Clock Options by clicking that pane of the control panel. The dialog shown in Figure 8-2 opens.

Clock Options

As you can see from Figure 8-2, SuperClock! is crammed with options. Start with the first panel. The first set, Clicking on the clock, tells SuperClock! how you want it to react to being clicked.

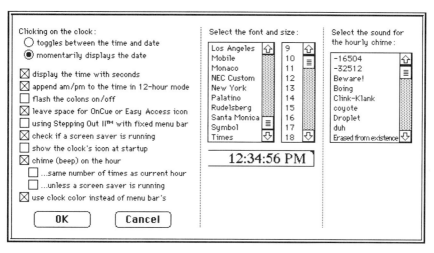

Figure 8-2 Clock Options Window

If you want the clock to change its display from time to date when clicked, select the first radio button. If you'd rather it showed the date for only a moment before returning to the time display, click on the second radio button.

Beneath the Clicking on the clock options are eleven check boxes that let you further customize SuperClock! Select those that give you the clock you need.

Selecting the "chime (beep) on the hour" option has two immediate effects. First, it activates the two check boxes beneath it, letting you set SuperClock! to chime the same number of times as the hour (three chimes for 3 o'clock) and to deactivate the hourly chime if a screen saver (like After Dark) is running. The right pane of the dialog has the familiar list of sounds from your System. Clicking on a sound's name selects it and also plays that sound.

The final box, when checked, lets you specify what color you want the clock to be—it doesn't have to be black if you have a color monitor. Selecting this box calls up the color wheel dialog you used to select colors in Chapter Two. You can select and tweak your clock's color the same way you did your Mac's highlight color. Go for something that coordinates with your desktop or something that stands out so you can easily tell time at a glance.

In the center pane of the dialog, you can select the clock's display typeface and size. This option is a real boon for folks with tired eyes. Try combinations of typeface and size until you find the one that suits you.

A word of warning, though: depending on the applications you run and how crowded your menu bar gets, a large font can crowd SuperClock! right off your menu bar. A big clock that you can't see at all is just as useless as a tiny clock you can't read.

In the crowded menu department, System 7 users have an additional problem: the ever-present Balloon Help icon. I'll dispose of that in a minute. First, let's finish configuring your clock.

When you're done setting all the clock options, click on the **OK** button to return to the SuperClock! control panel.

Timer Options

Clicking the second pane of the control panel calls up SuperClock's timer options (shown in Figure 8-3). Here you can specify whether SuperClock! counts up to or down from a specified time, how it lets you know when the time has run out, and what it does next.

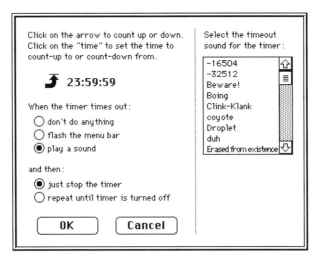

Figure 8-3. SuperClock! Timer Options

The instructions in this dialog are perfectly clear. Click on the arrow to set the direction SuperClock! counts, up or down. Click on the time display and enter the amount of time you want SuperClock! to count.

When the timer runs out, SuperClock! does one of three things: nothing, flashes the menu bar, or plays a sound. Click on the radio button beside the option you want to enable. If you select the sound option, be sure to select a sound from the scroll box.

After you've told SuperClock! how to let you know you've run out of time, you have to tell it what to do next. Do you want it to sound the alarm (or flash the menu bar) once and stop, or do you want it to keep flashing until you open its control panel and shut it off? Click on the radio button next to the option you want. Personally, I keep the repeat option selected. A subtle alarm is useless to me.

When you have the timer configured the way you want, click on the **OK** button.

To use SuperClock's timer, just double-click on the clock. It changes to the stopwatch shown in Figure 8-4. Click on the stopwatch, and the clock counts up or down the amount of time you specified in the control panel.

Figure 8-4. SuperClock! in Timer Mode

This feature is especially handy if you use online services with hourly rates. Decide before you log on how much time (and money) you're going to spend and set the timer to match. When you log on, start the timer counting down. When the alarm goes off, you log off and you've stayed within your budget. You can also use it to time long distance calls or anything else that needs timing.

Alarm Options

Clicking on the third pane of SuperClock's control panel opens the Alarm Options dialog shown in Figure 8-5. Here you can set SuperClock! to go off like an alarm clock.

To set the time you want the alarm to go off, click on the dialog's time display. To activate the alarm, click on the alarm

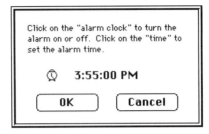

Figure 8-5. SuperClock's Alarm Options

clock icon. It's set to go when the little lines (what cartoonists call *agitrons,* because they show agitation) appear over the bell.

When the clock hits the time you've set, SuperClock! beeps with your system beep. Simultaneously, the ⌘ menu icon changes into an agitated alarm clock and flashes until you turn the alarm off.

Elbow Room with NoBalloonMenu— System 7 Only

As I said earlier, a big clock that you can't see is just as useless as a tiny clock you can't read. If you're running System 7, the icon for the Balloon Help menu takes up valuable menu bar real estate even with MICN installed. Once you've learned a program, how often are you going to need help balloons? Not often, probably not until you need to learn another program that utilizes Balloon Help. In the meantime, the balloon icon is in the way.

NoBalloonMenu, a freeware INIT (or extension) by Australian Malcom Davidson, completely removes the Balloon Help icon from the menu bar, giving SuperClock! a little elbow room.

To use it, simply click-and-drag the NoBalloonMenu icon from its folder in the System 7 Only folder in the Mac/Mine Apps folder and drop it on top of your closed System Folder. Your Mac will prompt you with the message "Extensions should be stored in the Extensions folder...OK?" Click on **OK** and your system will finish copying NoBalloonMenu. When it's done, restart your Mac.

When you arrive at your desktop, the balloon is gone, popped, burst, deflated into nonexistence, and everything in your menu bar can breathe a little more freely.

If you ever need Balloon Help back, just drag the NoBalloonMenu icon out of your System Folder and restart your Mac. The balloon is back.

The combination of SuperClock! and NoBalloonMenu is dynamite. It not only gives you the clock you need where you need it, but also makes use of space that would sit idle most of the time you use your Macintosh.

SuperClock!, in addition to its innate practicality and abundance of useful features, gives you the opportunity to do a good deed (see Figure 8-6). Who could ask for anything more?

Figure 8-6. A Nice Thing

Ted Turner's Revenge: Colorize

In which enraged Ted Turner fans use Colorize to add clashing colors to the menus, windows, and dialog boxes of classic black-and-white applications.

It seems to be one of life's annoying rules—you know the kind I mean: As soon as you bought a Beta video cassette recorder, VHS kicked its butt. When you discovered this fabulous new restaurant, it went out of business. And when you shell out big bucks for a color monitor, you learn how few applications really make use of color.

Well, you can't do anything about the Beta/VHS thing, and you sure can't force a restaurant back on its feet, but you *can* make better use of your color monitor by adding color to applications that otherwise neglect it.

Colorize (shareware, $5) by Neal Trautman lets you add color to boring black-and-white applications. No, it won't turn a black-and-white paint program into a color paint program, but it will add your choice of colors to windows, dialog boxes, and menu bars in just about any application.

Colorization Theory

You know the theory behind colorizing movies. Computers are used to digitally color the frames of black-and-white movies so they look more like modern films. It doesn't change the film's plot or action, but it does change its appearance and feeling. The change of feeling, or atmosphere, is what upsets most people about movie colorization, aside from the fact that the color looks completely unnatural.

The theory behind colorizing a computer application is similar. Colorize opens an application's resource fork (see Chapter Twelve for more information on Macintosh resources) and changes how the application displays data. Colorization in no way alters the basic operation of an application, just the way it looks on the computer screen. I don't think anyone will be as upset with you for adding color to your copy of Microsoft Works, as they would if Ted Turner colorized *Citizen Kane*.

Using Colorize

As a precaution, use Colorize only on a duplicate, never the original, of any application. Colorize is fairly harmless as utilities go, but things can go wrong, so why gamble. Also, if you are running MultiFinder or Finder 7, do *not* try to colorize an open application. If the application is running, close it before using Colorize. If you don't, Colorize will bomb out on you.

Colorize is a stand-alone application. To start it up, double-click on its icon in the Colorize folder inside the Mac/Mine Apps folder on your hard drive.

When Colorize opens, the first thing you'll see is the dialog in Figure 9-1, which prompts you to select an application to colorize.

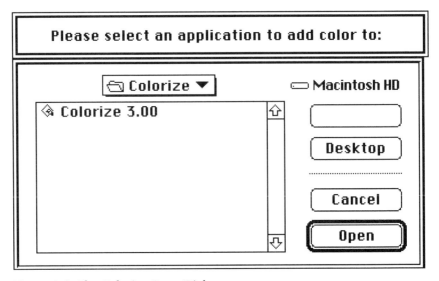

Figure 9-1. The Colorize Open Dialog

Use this dialog to navigate to the backup copy of an application on your hard drive, or on a disk in your floppy drive, that you want to add color to.

When you've selected and opened the application you want to colorize, you are presented with the main Colorize dialog (shown in Figure 9-2).

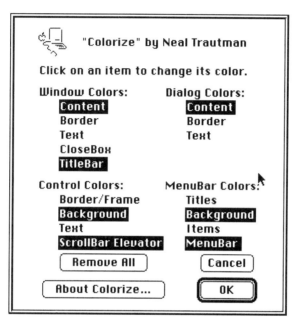

Figure 9-2. Colorize Dialog

Colorize gives you four main choices for adding color. You can add color to windows, dialogs, window and dialog controls, and the menu bar.

Window Colors

Under the Window Colors heading, you can change the color of the window's Content, Border, Text, CloseBox, and TitleBar. They are all options that affect a window's general appearance.

The window Content is the background color. Normally it's plain white.

The Border, normally black, is the box that frames the window.

Text, regularly black, includes only items that are actually part of the window. Text, like a scrollable file list, that's read from a disk or hard drive and can change each time the window opens, remains black.

The CloseBox option colorizes the box in the upper left corner of all windows that you click on to close that window.

The TitleBar is the thick top border that shows the title of the disk or folder the window represents.

Colorize has a problem coloring title bars and close boxes in System 7, because System 7's Color control panel wants to do it. The conflict doesn't make the colorized application crash or do anything nasty, but the color you applied may not show up.

Control Colors

The four options you can change under the Control Colors heading are Border/Frame, Background, Text, and ScrollBar Elevator. They are all options related to functions in windows and dialogs that you click on to select.

The Border/Frame option colorizes the outline of buttons, radio buttons, and check boxes.

The Background color is the interior color of buttons, radio buttons, and check boxes.

The Text option changes the color of text inside buttons.

The Scrollbar Elevator option adds color to the outline of the application's scroll bars.

Dialog Colors

The Dialog Colors option allows you to select new colors for dialog box Content, Borders, and Text.

Content is the dialog box background color. Border is the frame that forms the dialog box. Text is the text that is an actual part of the dialog. As with the Window Colors Text option, text that can change each time you open a dialog, like a directory of files read from a disk, remains black.

MenuBar Colors

The MenuBar heading gives you four options to colorize: Titles, Backgrounds, Items, and MenuBar.

The Titles option colors the text of menu names, like File and Edit. Background colors the background of each menu when it's open. Items colors the menu text, like Open and Close under the File menu. MenuBar colors the menu bar's background.

Staying within the Lines

When you're ready to begin colorizing an application (that is, you've started Colorize, navigated to the application you want to color with the open dialog, and opened it), the rest is just a matter of point and click.

If you want to change the color of the window title bars in an application, just click on the word **TitleBar** under the Window Colors heading. You are presented with the color-wheel dialog shown in Figure 9-3. The Colorize color wheel has all the same functions and features of the system's color wheel.

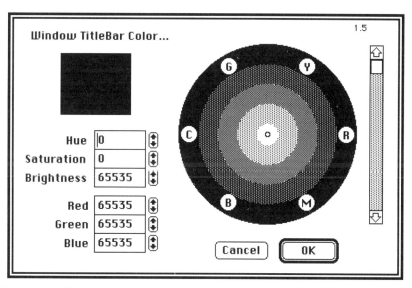

Figure 9-3. The Colorize Color Wheel

To change the intensity/darkness of the color wheel, use the scrollbar at the right of the wheel. Remember, the bottom setting of the scrollbar turns the wheel black, so if you want a livelier color, move the slider up.

When the color wheel reaches the shade you want, move the cursor onto the wheel. The cursor turns into a hollow circle. Position the circular cursor on the color you want to use and click to select it. The new color appears in the top half of the color box on the left side of the dialog.

You can further adjust the color by using the brightness scrollbar, or you can enter new values in the Hue/Saturation/Brightness and Red/Green/Blue boxes below the color box.

When you're satisfied with the new color, click on the **OK** button, and you'll be returned to the main Colorize dialog. Notice that the word TitleBar is now rendered in the new color. That makes it easy to remember what options you've changed and what colors you've used, if you want to keep things color coordinated.

Repeat the process for each of the colorizing features you want to use.

When you're done adding color, click on the **OK** button at the bottom of the Colorize Dialog. Your changes are added to the application, and Colorize returns you to the Open dialog. You can open another application and add color to it, or you can click on the **Cancel** button to quit Colorize.

That's all there is to it. The next time you open the application you altered, its dull black-and-white dialogs and windows will be in glorious color.

Undoing Colorize

Oh, ack! That was my reaction to the first color job I'd done on an application. Ugly? You'd better be glad this book's illustrations are in black and white. Who knew I had such bad taste? I could design pants for golfers.

If you create a really hideous mess—and it's easy to do—don't worry. None of the changes is permanent. You can fix things one of two ways.

You can reopen Colorize, select the garish application, and redo some of the offending colors by selecting new colors for each option, one at a time.

Or you can click on the **Remove All** button, which removes all the color you've added to an application. All of it. When you opt to remove all of your changes, Colorize will ask if you're sure you want to remove all the colors. Click on **OK** and your application is returned to pristine black and white. You can then reselect the application and start from scratch.

Colorizing Tips

Avoid very light shades. Some of the lighter colors, like yellow and green, may turn up as white in your application. Not a good color for a button or check box—you can't click on what you can't see.

Practice makes perfect. There is some variation between the color you choose on the color wheel and the color that appears in your application. Dark colors get darker, light colors may fade to white. With a little practice, you'll learn to compensate for these variations.

Don't get too carried away. You *can* add color to every single option available in Colorize. I know, I tried it. That was what made me say *Oh, ack!* and start over.

Be careful in System 7. If you add color to a title bar or close box and System 7 overrides your change, go in and undo it. Leaving it alone probably won't do anything bad to your Mac, but why dedicate time and memory to a change you can't see on the screen?

Let your taste be your guide. With Colorize and a little time, you can liven up all your boring black-and-white applications with spots of color. It will certainly relieve some of the tedium of doing spreadsheets and data entry.

Peeping Through Windows

In which Tom's primal snooping urge is satisfied by an INIT that lets him peer into hidden windows without disturbing the desktop or leaving finger-prints. He says, "It's more fun than going through people's medicine cabinets."

Did you ever wonder why, when the concept of working in a window is so convenient, it gets so much more difficult when you have two, three, or more open at the same time? It's like some kind of Murphy's law for windows: The convenience drops in direct proportion to the number of windows you have open at the time.

If you've ever found yourself clicking wildly around your desktop, trying to bring a particular window to the front, you're going to love **WindowShade**. Even if you haven't had many window difficulties, you'll still love it. Besides being practical, it's fun.

WindowShade (freeware) by Robert Johnston is one of those control panels that makes you wonder why Apple never included something like it in the Mac's System software. Elegantly simple, it allows you to roll up any standard window (like a window shade) so you can get a look at what's behind it.

Installing WindowShade

Since WindowShade is a control panel, installation is easy. Just open the WindowShade folder inside the Mac/Mine Apps folder on your hard drive. Click-drag the WindowShade icon into your open System Folder (System 6.0.X), or into your open Control Panels folder (System 7), and restart your Mac.

Of course, if you're running System 7, you can just drag the WindowShade icon onto your closed System Folder. When the system prompts you with the message: "Control Panels need to be stored in the Control Panels folder...OK?"click on **OK**. The system will finish copying the file. Restart your Mac by selecting **Restart** from the Special menu.

When you restart, you'll see the WindowShade icon at the bottom of your screen with all the other startup icons.

Using WindowShade

Using WindowShade is simple. To roll up a window, all you do is double-click on its title bar; the window gets sucked up into it like an old fashioned window shade. Get it? Figures 10-1 and 10-2 illustrate a screen before and after WindowShade is used.

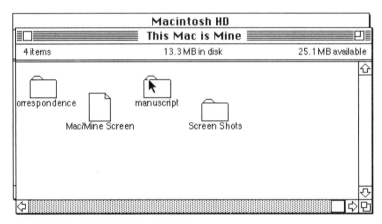

Figure 10-1 Two Windows before WindowShade

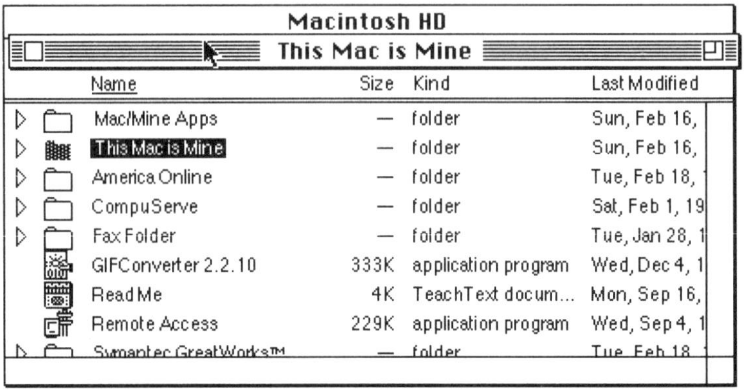

Figure 10-2 Two Windows after WindowShade

The double-click is the default setting, but you can configure it so that windows roll up with one, two, or three clicks. The same number of clicks unfurls the windows.

You can also add a modifying key (the Control, Option, or Command key) in combination with the number of clicks. Depending on how you work, adding the modifier can prevent you from accidentally rolling up windows.

To configure WindowShade, open its control panel (shown in Figure 10-3) by the method appropriate to your version of the System software. Clicking on the **About** button shows you the copyright information. The middle pane sets the number of clicks it takes to roll up the window. Just click on the appropriate radio button for the number you want, or click on **Off** to disable WindowShade.

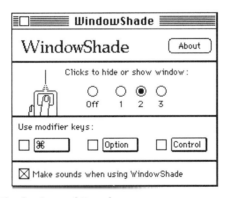

10-3. WindowShade Control Panel

Beneath that, you can select a modifying key, as mentioned earlier. Just click the appropriate check box. If you'd rather do without a modifying key, ignore this panel.

Last, but not least, you can add sound to the opening and closing of windows. Select the check box labeled **Make sounds when using WindowShade**. Now, these aren't customizable sounds (unless you want to try getting clever with SoundMover), but they're cool sounds. Selecting the check box just toggles the sounds on or off.

Unlike changes made on some control panels, the changes made to WindowShade take effect immediately. You don't have to restart every time you reconfigure it. That's especially handy if you work with windows differently from program to program. If your regular two clicks–no modifier setting closes windows accidentally in Aldus PageMaker, for example, you can change the settings to two clicks with the Option key, without having to restart and reopen all the applications and files you already have open.

WindowShade Tips and Tricks

If you hold down the Command key, you can click on the title bar of a window *behind* the active window. That rolls up the window without bringing it forward on the desktop. That's a handy feature if you have windows three, four, or more layers deep on the desktop. Instead of bringing each window forward to examine its contents, you can roll up each in turn until you find the file or folder you need.

WindowShade works on almost all windows—I say almost because, even though it worked with every window I've tried it on, there may be some it cannot close. On the other hand, it will even roll up some things that you don't think of as windows. For example, you can click on the Calculator's title bar, and the Calculator will roll up. If you have an odd shaped window and aren't sure if WindowShade can deal with it, try. When in doubt, check it out. The worst thing that can happen is nothing.

WindowShade is stable and reliable, but you may run into some difficulties. Occasionally, when you're using WindowShade with SndControl (described in Chapter 4), the two programs may squabble over which has control of your Mac's Sound Control Panel. Finder sounds set with SndControl, or WindowShade's opening and closing sounds, may become distorted, play slowly, or not play at all. The problem is easy to resolve. You can either turn off the "Make sounds when using WindowShade" option by clicking on the check box to remove the check mark, or you can reduce the number of Finder functions SndControl adds sound to.

To eliminate sounds associated with Finder functions in SndControl, open the SndControl Control Panel. Click on the radio button beside the function you wish to silence, then scroll to the top of the sound listing. The first entry is a blank line. Click on the blank line to select it. Now there is no sound associated with the selected Finder function. Repeat the process for each function you want to silence. See Chapter 4 if you need more information on selecting and deselecting sounds or Finder functions in SndControl.

WindowShade also appears to conflict with Shiva NetModem's Shiva Config INIT. For information on resolving INIT conflicts, see Chapter 12.

WindowShade comes in very handy when you're moving files between windows, or just for keeping track of what you actually have open on the desktop. When combined with AltWDEF (in Chapter Five), you have almost total control over your windows.

Once you get used to working with WindowShade and AltWDEF, you'll wonder how you ever got along without them.

Drop Me a Note

In which Mrs. Robinson exclaims, "You don't call, you never write, and you never tell me what you're feeling." Ben responds by dropping colorful icon notes all over her desktop. They say only one word: Plastic. For the moment, she is satisfied.

I always feel like Andy Rooney when I say this, but…did you ever wonder why Apple never included a way to drop yourself a note on the desktop? If they're going to go all the way with this desktop image, they should have looked at a real desktop. Mine's littered will all kinds of notes and reminders. Places to go, people to see, and things to do. Ever since the folks at 3M introduced Post-it™ Note Pads, even the walls aren't safe from my scribbles to myself.

So why doesn't the Mac play along? The Note Pad DA is okay—if you remember to check it. I don't. I need something a little more immediate and startling. Something in the "if it was a snake, it would'a bit me" line.

Russ Coffman's done it up right with his own version of Post-it Notes called **Desktop Notes**.

The Desktop Notes utility is unusual: it isn't shareware or freeware, it's *beerware*. If you keep and use it, you're honor bound to hoist one in Russ's name. Being a Texan, Russ specifies a bottle of Lone Star beer, or your local equivalent (though I imagine a soft drink will do for underaged folks or those who don't like beer).

There are 42 notes included in the Desktop Notes folder. If you're running System 7, your system can display color icons. Desktop notes will appear in glorious color and are immediately noticed whenever you are at the desktop. If you can't use color icons, they appear in black and white. Even in black and white, they're hard to miss, especially if you put them near the trash or another frequently used desktop icon.

How to Use Desktop Notes

At first glance, they look like just about any other icons you've ever seen (Figure 11-1), but Desktop Notes are neither fish nor fowl: They're more than just icons, yet they're not quite applications. They don't actually do anything. If you double-click on one, your Mac will go through the motions of opening an application, but quits right after. They're harmless.

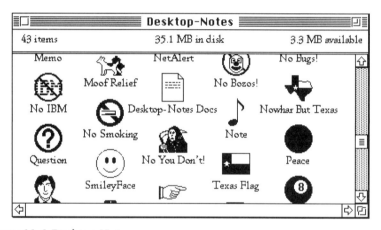

Figure 11-1 Desktop Notes

To use them, just copy one or more of them onto your desktop. Pressing the Option key while you click-and-drag the note to the desktop places a copy there, not the original.

Put them where you'll see them, otherwise they won't do you much good. Near the trash icon is a good space, as shown in Figure 11-2. You can even put notes to yourself in folders and on floppy disks, as long as you're using View by Icon or View by Small Icon.

The notes's name provides your message space. Add your message the same way you would rename any other file or folder.

Figure 11-2. Desktop Notes in Action

Select the Desktop note by clicking on it. When its name is high-lighted for editing, just type in your message.

Use one or two, or use a bunch. I have them littering my desk-top with reminders like "Check Email" and "Deadline 2/28," but also with notes as mundane as "Change Cat Litter." Some I just leave the way they are. "No Bozos" pretty much says it all, and think of the fun you can have throwing John Sculley in the trash (you know you *want* to). Maybe someone will do a Bill Gates icon.

If the few words that fit in the icon's name space aren't enough, you can leave a more detailed note. When the icon is selected (by clicking on it once) choose the **Get Info** command from the File menu. You can enter as much explanatory text as the Comment box will hold. Enter more than four lines, though, and you'll have to scroll down to read it all.

Warning! If you use the Comments box for messages, do not rebuild your desktop (by pressing Command-Option at startup) with Desktop Notes scattered around. Rebuilding the desktop erases all Comment files, not just for the notes, but for any file or folder with comments. Kiss them goodbye.

Let's face it, though, sooner or later you *will* have to rebuild your desktop. Some programs recommend or require it as part of the installation process (Microsoft Excel for one). It's also a good idea to rebuild your desktop from time to time just to keep it tidy, the same way it's a good idea to check a car's oil between tune ups. When you have to rebuild your desktop, move any Desktop Notes with comments entered in their Get Info boxes off of the desktop and onto a disk. Restart your Mac and hold down the Command and Option keys to rebuild the desktop. When it's finished and you're back in the Finder, restore your Desktop Notes to the desktop and your comments will be intact.

Networks and Such

AppleShare users and LAN managers, rejoice! You will find Desktop Notes especially useful. They were originally written for use on a network. They can be dropped around the host/server's desktop and left as warnings and reminders to other folks as they share files. You'll notice that many of the messages are already geared toward network reminders ("Please Purge Files" and "Net Alert" to mention two).

If you tire of these Desktop Notes and are handy with ResEdit, you can create your own (or just edit the existing ones). Instructions are included in the Desktop Notes Docs file hiding among the notes. If you don't know what ResEdit is, you can find out more about it in Chapter Twelve, Frankenstein's Mac.

If you come up with some new ones, drop me a note.

Frankenstein's Mac

In which Janet complains to Dr. Frank that his Macintosh is getting out of control. He cries, "I didn't make it for YOU!" and gives her the information she needs to customize and control her own Mac.

So, where do we go from here? Well, to be perfectly honest, I don't know. There are *billions and billions* of things you can do to customize the Mac's interface to your own likes and needs. Okay, maybe hundreds, but still there are lots of things to try to get your Mac just the way you like it. Your only limitations are the amount of patience you have, the amount of time and money you're prepared to spend searching out and trying new software, and your Mac's memory.

Memory

A word about memory: *ouch!*

Every INIT and CDEV you load to soup up your Mac takes up memory. First it takes up room on your hard drive, then it sneaks chunks of memory from your System Heap (that's where unused system memory hangs out until called for). You can find out how much memory your system is using by selecting **About This Macintosh** from the ◆ menu (**About the Finder** under System 6). See Figure 12-1.

Memory under System 6.0.X was tight enough, but if you're running System 7 it's even tighter. System 7 is so large, you can hardly fit a fully functional copy on a high-density disk. Stripped down (with features you don't use pulled out of the System Folder)

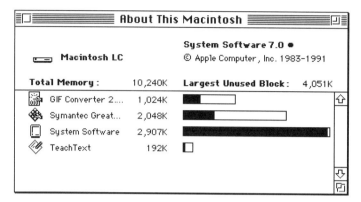

Figure 12-1. Memory Allocation from the About This Macintosh Window

it still uses about 1,100K of system memory. That's with a minimal 16K RAM cache and before any INITs or anything else is added. Each startup item takes a little bit more of your system's memory, leaving you with less to open and use applications.

There is a System 7 **Tune-up** available from Apple, which improves memory management for folks running System 7 with 2 megabytes of memory. It's also supposed to improve file sharing for network users and printing speed if you use an Apple printer. Check with your local authorized Apple dealer, Macintosh User Group (MUG), or online service for a copy.

Even with the Tune-up, the final word about memory is *More*.

If you plan to continue your search for the perfect custom interface, you need at least 4 megabytes of RAM (2 for your system and 2 for everything else you want to do). If you can afford to buy more than that, go ahead. The way applications keep sucking up more memory, you won't be sorry.

Remember to turn on System 7's 32-bit addressing feature with the Memory Control Panel if you install a total of more than 8 megabytes of memory. Otherwise your Mac can't use the balance over 8 megs. Mac Classic, SE, Plus, and Portable owners can't use 32-bit addressing because their 6800 central processing units can't handle it.

Mac II, IIx, IIcx, and SE/30 owners can't use 32-bit addressing because their read-only memory chips (ROMs) aren't compatible with it. They aren't 32-bit "clean." You can side-step the problem by using Connectix's MODE 32, which Apple Computer is distributing free to owners of afflicted Macs.

You can get your free copy from Apple's authorized dealers, MUGs, and online services. Apple is offering refunds to folks who bought MODE 32 before they admitted 32-bit defeat and began distributing it for free. See the Resource list at the back of the book for more information.

Frankenstein Lives!

Frankenstein's monster turned on him in the end and killed him in nine out of ten of the movies. Of course, that never stopped them from bringing old Dr. F. back for sequels.

If, like Dr. Frankenstein, you're going to continue trying to bring your Mac to customized life (so to speak), you need to take some basic precautions. You probably won't have an angry mob of villagers pounding on your door with torches and pitchforks, but you could wind up waking the neighbors with your screams of frustration.

Once you increase your Mac's memory, you'll eliminate annoying "Out of (buy more?) Memory" messages. Then you'll eventually have to deal with an INIT conflict.

INIT Management 101

Not all INITs get along. Sometimes they fight over memory allocation. Sometimes they try and take control of the same part of the system. Sometimes they're just badly written and crash for no apparent reason.

When an INIT gives you trouble, don't just chuck it in the trash. Sometimes you can resolve the problem by changing the order in which it loads. First you have to find out which INITs are causing the problem.

Half of the job's done for you. One of the clashing INITs will be the last one you installed. The hard part is finding the one it conflicts with. You could just randomly pull INITs out of your system and restart your Mac to see if the problem reoccurs. Unless you're very lucky, however, you'll wind up chasing your own tail. Don't panic. There is an easier way.

- Remove all the INITs from your System Folder (or Extensions Folder) except for the new one. Click-drag them into an empty folder on your hard drive (call it Idle INITS or something). Restart your Mac by selecting **Restart** from the Special menu.

- If the INIT crashes alone, you've got a bad INIT. Trash it.

- If it starts up normally, add one of your other INITs. Restart.

- If it starts up normally, add another and restart. Continue adding INITs and restarting until you duplicate the conflict. You've identified the culprit.

- Try changing the INITs' loading order to resolve the problem. (Add a ! or an A to the beginning of the INIT's name so it comes first alphabetically). Failing that, add a • or a ~ to the beginning of its name so it loads last. Restart your Mac and cross your fingers.

- Try restarting with each of the troublesome INITs loading first and last. If neither order solves the problem, decide which INIT you're willing to live without or try an INIT manager.

INIT Management 201

There are a variety of commercial INIT management programs, as well as shareware and freeware utilities available from a number of sources (mentioned later in this chapter). I use **INIT Manager**, a commercial control panel device (CDEV) from Baseline Publishing. It has served me pretty well.

INIT managers let you turn one INIT or a group of INITs on or off as you start your Mac. They also let you change their loading order without having to rename files.

If you intend to get serious about customizing your Mac, it would be well worth your time and money to invest in an INIT manager of some sort, commercial, freeware, or shareware.

The Pursuit of the Perfect Desktop

Once you've got the memory to use them, and an electronic whip-and-chair to keep them in line, where can you find more INITs and CDEVs? A lot of places.

Books and Disks

You can start with other books like this one. *Stupid Mac Tricks* and *Son of Stupid Mac Tricks* by Bob LeVitus are collections of applications, INITs, and control panels with a decidedly silly bent ("Reagan's Watching" is more lifelike than the real thing). Check your favorite bookstore or software retailer for these and other book–disk combinations.

User Groups

Join a Macintosh user group (MUG), a collective of Mac users who meet to exchange ideas, information, and, of course, shareware. There are MUGs all over the place.

On the east coast, you can start with the Boston Computer Society. On the west, the Berkeley Mac User Group. You don't have to live in Berkeley or Boston to be a member—folks join from all around the world. Many MUGs publish newsletters chock-full of useful information. BMUG's is especially good. It should be called a news-*book*. The Spring '92 issue contains over 450 pages of news you can use.

If you're somewhere between the coasts, consult your nearest authorized Apple dealer for the name of a user group in your area. You can also call Apple for the same information. See the Resource list at the back of this book for more information.

Membership in a MUG costs anywhere from $20 to $60 a year, and membership usually gets you a subscription to the group's newsletter, access to libraries of software, discounts on commercial software and hardware, and all kinds of other good stuff. MUGs are well worth joining.

Modem Operandi

When you add a modem to your Mac, the electronic world is yours. A modem (a contraction of modulating and demodulating) is a device that converts information from your computer into sounds that can be transmitted over telephone lines to a computer at another location. The receiving computer's modem translates the sound back to usable information at that end.

It literally puts the world at your fingertips. You can call a friend's computer and share files or type messages back and forth. It gives you a mini-network.

You can log onto an electronic bulletin board service (BBS), which gives you access to that system's message boards, file libraries, and chat areas where you and other users can meet "face to face" and talk in real time. BBSs are usually small, local, and run by computer hobbyists in their spare time. Services vary from board to board, as do the number of users. Some can accept only one caller at a time, others have multiple phone lines for multiple users.

Membership fees run from free to about $50 per year. Some boards have a free level with limited services that you can access for an hour a day without charge. To get to more advanced features (like the file libraries and chat rooms) you must pay a subscription fee.

The trouble with some BBSs is that, since many are run as hobbies, they come and go quickly. As people gain and lose interest in running them, old boards fold and new ones take their place. That makes it hard to keep track of them.

The great thing about them is their diversity. There are as many different kinds of boards as there are people running them. You can find boards dedicated to gaming, hobbies, interests, lifestyles, and just about anything else you can think of.

To locate a BBS in your area, ask at your local authorized Apple dealer or MUG meeting.

You may want to consider joining a national electronic service like America Online or CompuServe. These are commercial services that have thousands of members, dozens of special interest groups (SIGs), and often a software library and chat area for each

SIG. That's all in addition to basic services like electronic mail (e-mail) and bulletin boards.

Generally you pay a monthly fee for these major services, plus an hourly connection charge. The bill can add up fast. It's easy to lose track of time online, especially chatting or reading the boards. A stopwatch helps (or SuperClock! in its stopwatch mode).

All of the software on the *This Mac Is Mine* disk was downloaded from America Online. Many of the program authors use the service. It's easy to get in touch with them if you have a problem with their program.

Electronic bulletin boards, both local and national, are an endless source of customizing accessories for your Mac. You can find applications, INITs, DAs, CDEVs—the whole gamut of program types for your Mac—as well as graphic images, sounds, icons, and enormous information resources about your Mac and your favorite applications.

Many software and hardware companies (Apple included) maintain technical support areas online. They're convenient if you have a problem with their product, but also handy for finding out about program upgrades and new products.

You can get a free startup kit for America Online by calling 1-800-227-6364. Starter kits for CompuServe are available in computer and book stores. You'll also get information and/or software for these and many other services bundled with your modem.

With a modem and an online service (either local or national), you can keep your finger on the pulse of the electronic community.

Genetic Tinkertoys for Your Mac

If cosmetic changes, like those you've made here, aren't enough for you, you can get right down into the guts of your Macintosh with a handy little program called **ResEdit**. ResEdit is a resource editor from the folks at Apple. To understand how it works, you have to understand a little about how Macs work.

All the software that runs on your Mac is modular (like a component stereo). There's a data fork and a resource fork. In each fork there are small bundles of information your software needs in order to run. The data fork (if you haven't guessed) contains program data. The resource fork contains everything you see on your Mac's screen—menus, dialog boxes, windows, icons, everything. With ResEdit, you can alter everything you see on your Mac's screen by editing the appropriate resource.

You can do everything, from redrawing the trash can icon to adding new Command-key shortcuts to menus in the Finder or any other program. But be warned: ResEdit is powerful and, used carelessly, dangerous. Using ResEdit is like performing brain surgery on your Mac. Make the wrong move and your Mac is lobotomized.

ResEdit is free. You can get it from your local authorized Apple dealer, MUG, or online service. When you get it, though, there's no documentation. You're on your own. Luckily, there are a number of good books available on ResEdit.

One is *ResEdit Complete*, by Peter Alley and Carolyn Strange. It's a modular, learn-as-you-go book that comes with a copy of ResEdit. It's published by Addison-Wesley. They also handle the official Apple ResEdit manual.

BMUG publishes *Zen and the Art of Resource Editing*, edited by Derrick Schneider. It also comes with the current version of ResEdit (2.1.1 at this writing) and is chock-full of wild things you can do to your system.

Do yourself a favor—don't try resource editing without a manual. If you create a monster, you'll want to be able to drive a stake through its heart.

Last Things Last

On a personal note, I hope you enjoy using *This Mac Is Mine* as much as I enjoyed putting it together for you. I worry about that. Let me know.

Let me know, too, if you come across any really interesting customizing tools in your travels. I'm *always* interested. You can contact me a number of ways:

- c/o Addison-Wesley Publishing Company
  Trade Computer Books Division
  1 Jacob Way
  Reading, MA 01867
- on America Online: PIV
- on CompuServe: John Pivovarnick, 70713, 3554

Thanks for hanging out with me for a while. Let's do it again sometime.

Resource List

In which the author, tired of being a name-dropper, drops all his names at once, adding addresses and phone numbers for the software, services, and information sources mentioned in the rest of this book.

Just to save you a lot of time flipping around trying to find references to software, hardware, and information sources salted throughout *This Mac Is Mine*, the following is an alphabetical listing of products, services, and information sources mentioned in the text. These aren't recommendations, just information. I hope you find it useful.

Adobe Type Manager, an INIT that improves the appearance of display fonts onscreen and in output printed from non-PostScript printers. ATM is to be built into a future upgrade of System 7. It's available now (to System 7 users) for the price of shipping and handling ($7.50) by calling Adobe at 1-800-833-6687.

America Online, a commercial electronic information service for modem users. America Online, Inc., 8619 Westwood Center Dr., Vienna, VA 22182. 800-227-6364. Startup kits come bundled with many popular brands of modem.

BMUG (Berkeley Mac User's Group), a great west coast user group. BMUG, Inc., 1442A Walnut St., #62, Berkeley, CA 94709. 415-549-BMUG.

Boston Computer Society, another MUG, this time on the east coast. 617-367-8080.

CompuServe, a commercial electronic information service for modem users. You can locate a CompuServe startup kit in many bookstores and computer software retail stores, and through mail order companies.

Compact Pro, by Bill Goodman. Shareware ($25) compression utility. The program used to create the Mac/Mine Apps self-extracting archive on the *This Mac Is Mine* disk. Cyclos, P.O. Box 31417, San Francisco, CA 94131.

Disk Doubler, from Salient Software. Commercial compression utility. Salient Software, Inc., 124 University Ave., Palo Alto, CA 94301. 415-321-5375.

Disk First Aid, a disk repair/recovery application from Apple Computer. It's on your original System software disks.

Global Village TelePort/Fax, a small 2400 baud modem with send-fax capability. It's very small, plugs into an ADB port, leaving your modem or serial port free, and draws power through your Mac so there's no power cord. Very cool. Global Village Communications, Menlo Park, CA 94205. 415-329-0700.

GreatWorks v2.0, from Symantec. Eight integrated applications for the Mac, includes word processing, spreadsheet, database, chart, graph, paint, draw, and telecommunications modules. Symantec Corp., 10201 Torre Ave., Cupertino, CA 95014. 408-252-5700.

HyperCard 2.1, the original hyper-media tool, from Claris. Claris Corporation, 5201 Patrick Henry Drive, Box 58618, Santa Clara, CA 95052. 408-727-8227.

INIT Manager, from Baseline Publishing. Commercial program to control and analyze your INITs. Baseline Publishing, Inc., 1770 Moriah Woods Blvd., Suite 14, Memphis, TN 38117. 800-926-9677.

Local MUGs. You can get information on a Mac User Group in your area by calling Apple Computer at 1-800-538-9696.

MacPaint, the venerable Macintosh painting program, from Claris. Claris Corporation, 5201 Patrick Henry Drive, Box 58618, Santa Clara, CA 95052. 408-727-8227.

MacTools Deluxe, from Central Point Software. Commercial hard drive utility. Central Point Software, Inc., 15220 NW Greenbrier Parkway #200, Beaverton, OR 97006. 503-690-8080.

Mode 32, by Connectix. Software solution for Macs with "dirty" ROMs that don't allow 32-bit addressing. Apple is distributing it free of charge. Apple Computer, Inc., 20525 Mariani Ave., Cupertino, CA 95014. 800-776-2333.

ResEdit, from Apple Computer. The Macintosh resource editing utility. It's available from many online services and MUGs.

ResEdit Complete, by Alley and Strange. A step-by-step guide to ResEdit, this book includes a current version of the program. Published by Addison-Wesley Publishing Company. Check your local book or software store, or contact Retail Sales Group, Addison-Wesley Publishing Company, Route 128, Reading, MA 01867. 800-447-2226.

Silverlining, from La Cie. Commercial hard drive utility. La Cie, Ltd., 19552 SW 90th Court, Tualatin, OR 97062. 800-999-0143.

Son of Stupid Mac Tricks, by Bob LeVitus. A sequel to the very popular *Stupid Mac Tricks,* a book-disk combination of— well, stupid Mac tricks. Published by Addison-Wesley Publishing Company. Check your local book or software store, or contact Retail Sales Group, Addison-Wesley Publishing Company, Route 128, Reading, MA 01867. 800-447-2226.

Stupid Mac Tricks, by Bob LeVitus. A book-disk combination of— well, stupid Mac tricks. Published by Addison-Wesley Publishing Company. Check your local book or software store, or contact Retail Sales Group, Addison-Wesley Publishing Company, Route 128, Reading, MA 01867. 800-447-2226.

SwitchBoot INIT, a shareware INIT that lets you specify a startup drive at startup. It's available from many online services and user groups.

System Picker, a shareware INIT that lets you specify a startup drive at startup. It's available from many online services and user groups.

System 7 Tune-up, from Apple Computer. Improves memory management, printer speed, and file sharing. Available from Apple's usual distributors (authorized dealers, anointed user groups, and some online services) or direct: Apple Computer, Inc., 20525 Mariani Ave., Cupertino, CA 95014. 408-966-1010.

Zen and the Art of Resource Editing, edited by Derrick Schneider. A ResEdit guide that comes complete with a current copy of ResEdit. Available from BMUG (listed above).

If you just have to know

Because I know that this kind of thing means a lot to some people, here's the configuration of my own Mac.

- CPU: Macintosh LC, single Super Drive.
- System 7.0 with System 7 Tune-up.
- Memory: 10 megs RAM, 40 meg internal hard drive. I'm currently lusting after an 88 Meg removable media hard drive.
- Monitor: 12-inch Apple RGB.
- Keyboard: Datadesk 101E extended keyboard.
- Mouse: Logitech **TrackMan** track ball.
- Modem: Global Village **TelePort/Fax** (waiting for the upgrade to FullFax).
- The manuscript was written using Symantec's **GreatWorks** versions 1.0.2 and 2.0 (why do upgrades always come out in the *middle* of a project?).
- Screenshots were taken with Baseline's **Screenshot** and tinkered with in GreatWorks Paint module.

(I feel like there should be a naughty picture of me here, posed in front of my Mac, with a list of Turn Ons and Offs, and what the Mac of my dreams looks like. Woof.)

This Mac Is Mine
Compatibility Chart*

Program	Version	System Required	7 Compatible?	Required
AltWDEF	1.5.3	6.0.3 or later	Yes	
Colorize	3	6.0.7 or later	Yes	Color Mac
Desktop Notes	2	6.0.5 or later	Yes	
GIFConverter	2.2.10	6.0.5 or later	Yes	
Layout	1.9	6.0.5 or later	No	
MICN	1.2	6.0.5 or later	Yes	
NoBalloonMenu	1	7	Yes	
Sound Mover	1.74	6.0.5 or later	Yes	
StartupSndInit	1.4	6.0.5 or later	Yes	
SndControl	IBeep2	4.0.1—6.0.3	No	
	1.1.1	6.0.4 or later	No	
	1.1.3	7	Yes	
SuperClock!	3.9.1	6.0.5 or later	Yes	
WindowShade	1.2	6.0.5 or later	Yes	

*Note: a hard drive is required.